PLAN, ACT, IMPACT

A **PLAYBOOK** TO
ELEVATE YOUR **PERSPECTIVE** AND
UNSTICK YOUR **CAREER**

PLAN, ACT, IMPACT,

COLT McANLIS

LIONCREST
PUBLISHING

PLAN, ACT, IMPACT

A Playbook to Elevate Your Perspective and Unstick Your Career

ISBN   978-1-5445-1889-3 *Paperback*

978-1-5445-1888-6 *Ebook*

This book is dedicated to my children. It took me years to learn all this. I hope this book can help you master it quicker than I did, so that you might go on and do amazing things.

CONTENTS

INTRODUCTION

Joanna's smart. She's got the right education. She's driven and she's focused. She's so committed to her job she knows where all the light switches are—that's a side effect of being the first one in every morning and the last one to leave every night.

Yet, she was passed over for promotion, again, this year. Why?

Because, despite working hard and putting in all the hours, every six months Joanna's performance appraisal is summed up in three words: *not enough impact*.

For most of us, the concept of impact permeates our professional lives. It is the benchmark corporations measure against to decide where resources should flow and who gets rewarded for serving the corporate good. The value of making impact is immense. If the company you work for has an impact, its stock goes up. If your group makes an impact, it will get more funding. And, if *you* have impact, then promotions and pay raises will fall from the sky upon you.

However, the inverse is true, as we see with Joanna. And if she doesn't create enough impact this year, yet again, the chances are slim that she'll receive a promotion or raise. Even worse, should the company itself not make enough impact, then she may not even see the guarantee of a job.

But despite the constant murmur in the background about people making an impact and the perpetual push to do work that is impactful, it seems there's a lack of agreement over what impact means. If you ask ten different coworkers for their definition, you'll likely get ten different answers.

- It's about producing results.
- It's about doing what your manager wants.
- It's about doing the right thing, even if it's not what your manager wants.
- It's about customer happiness.
- It's about the bottom line.
- It's not about customer happiness but just doing enough to keep them paying.

The list could go on, but we think we made our point. Your

coworkers are likely as clueless as you are. So perhaps you could look beyond your coworkers to the managers, leaders, and owners of your company. Surely, they would know what impact is, right? After all, they are the ones doing the evaluating against it. They are the ones driving the big decisions based on making impact. And didn't they achieve their positions and rank by mastering it? They *must* be able to define it.

Sadly, that's just not always the case. We see confusion about impact play out at the upper levels, too. It frequently takes the form of a new VP joining the company and bringing with him a bold vision to turn things around. He makes daring moves. He gains resources, pivots the organization, keeps everyone on track, and drives them towards his vision. The pace is relentless, but he assures everyone it's going to be *huge*.

But then, the project goes nowhere. The impact isn't made. Everyone is burnt out. And eighteen months later, there's an announcement stating he's leaving the company to "spend more time with his family." The replacement steps in and unveils new grand plans while the rest of the division heaves a collective sigh and shakes their heads. "Here we go again," they think in unison.

Perhaps it only makes sense that many of us are frustrated. We cannot rely on our leaders to offer us a guide to sustain impact or on our management to give us a straight answer on what impact is, yet every twelve months, we sit in a room and hear them lecture us on how we didn't create enough of it. Meanwhile, some of our peers seem to have it down.

We watch them get promoted again and again with a natural skepticism. From our perspective, they seem to be doing the same work we are but getting the right kinds of credit. What do they know that we don't? Is it a secret handshake? The right presentation template? Did they download a premium font? Or is it something more nefarious, like being drinking buddies with the boss?

Like it or not, it appears there is an "in" club where all the members seem to have impact down to a science. We've all known someone on their roster: a rising-star coworker perfectly aligned with company goals and tapped into the right resources. Passionate about what they do, they have a series of successful endeavors and they rocket up the ladder. People like Joanna, meanwhile, are left spinning their wheels in the proverbial dust tracks.

I was a member of the impact club early in my career. Then I was kicked out—or rather, I wandered out. I wish I could say my departure was because I never mastered the secret handshake or that I didn't follow the directions given by the underground podcast. But the truth is, I never really knew I was in the club to begin with, nor understood what it took to stay in there.

See, I joined the club through grit and dumb luck. And once inside, I didn't know the rules I was expected to play by. So, when I got booted, I really had no idea what caused the change.

The good news is that I am back in the club, this time with intention. Finding my way back reads like a badly written detective novel, but in short: I focused on figuring out why some people were consistently successful and some were not. I analyzed why my managers and executives would get obsessed with goals that only wasted time and money, and I discovered that those patterns of behavior that led to a lack of impact were prevalent, regardless of what company I was looking at.

I even took a long look at my own past to figure out what I did right (and wrong). After quite a bit of research, questions, hordes of misfires, and perhaps too many bottles of whiskey, I finally stumbled across what I was looking for. It had been right in front of me all along, I just didn't recognize it. I found the art of making impact.*

---

* To be clear, there's not really a secret Impact Society, or a handshake, or anything. But if there were, it would be the title to a totally cool detective novel, right?

MAKING IMPACT

Over the past decade, I've had the pleasure of being able to mentor peers and consult with companies, which besides being fulfilling in its own right, provided quite a bit of insight into the behavior patterns and anti-patterns that go into making impact.

> Behavior patterns that lead to the *right* goals being targeted and achieved lead to making impact. Conversely, anti-patterns either lead to the *wrong* goals or they enable unimpactful actions.

After witnessing many anti-patterns, I can categorize them into three main camps. First (and most common) is getting caught in the quagmire of focusing on actions and work that "feel" right or that "seem" right, but in the end have no ability to create measurable results that matter to anyone. Joanna, from above, specialized in that kind of work. Second, are actions that create impressive impact but no one signed off their approval saying those specific results were wanted. And the third set of anti-patterns involves putting in massive amounts of time and effort only to create unintended consequences that are so large or so numerous, that you can't see the impact among all the chaos that's created.

In short, for folks in the not-making-impact group, the anti-patterns involved encouraged them to put in high effort but the outcomes were either unwanted or net negative. Interestingly, I also noticed there was a cyclical nature to anti-pattern behaviors that seemed to get folks in this group stuck without a clear sense of how to break their habits. Instead, they'd often find blame in other directions, only to move on and follow the same failures as before, despite the often-quoted definition of insanity.

The idea of doing things that feel right, or taking actions that seem right, and even playing the blame game are all symptomatic of what I discovered is the prevalent driving factor behind the non-impact group. Their behaviors were *emotionally* driven and therefore often detrimental. They were more prone to giving up, of making mountains out of molehills, to pivoting their careers in directions they didn't want them to go, and in general, spending a lot of time without getting a lot done.

Meanwhile, the impact-makers had patterns of behavior of their own, as perhaps expected, theirs were well defined. At the core, members of this group tended to have a big vision and a clear goal. Having a defined goal gave them energy and the ability to focus despite what was going on around them. That clarity of vision then gave them a sense of grit and determination. While embracing the passion to reach a goal, they kept their emotions in check as they spent a large amount of time planning. They researched what was needed to reach their goals so well, that they knew where things could go sideways and made contingencies to address them should they happen.

With these traits, the impact group continued to achieve higher and higher results. While the non-impact folks wallowed in trials and tribulations, the impact-group followed a cycle that perpetually ramped upwards. With each success and failure, they added to their tools and knowledge base so that future errors and snags along the way to their next goal would be easily overcome. They reveled in learning from mistakes and took pride in getting better. The folks who were masters, or experts in this space, were amazing to watch. In a few moments, they could gather all the information they needed, then with a year's worth of context in their minds, make accurate, on-the-spot decisions that resulted in huge impact. This led to a clear observation: making impact was a skill that can be perpetually honed.

That's an important thing to realize: these folks weren't born into the making-impact club the way Simba was born into ruling everything the light touches. They earned their way into it. They've got stories of trials and tribulations and about how each success was built upon their prior lessons learned.

So there's good news here: making impact is a skill you can learn. You have to train yourself to be good at it, but once you do, you'll have full access to the impact-makers club. The even better news is that's what you'll learn in this book.

MAKING IMPACT PLAYBOOK

In Part 1, we begin laying the basic groundwork for the Playbook by discussing what you might be doing that is preventing you from making impact. We'll discuss goals in Chapter 1: what bad ones look like, how to choose the right ones, and why it's important that you do so. Then, in Chapter 2, you'll have an opportunity to discover the anti-patterns you might be engaging in that hinder your ability to make impact. Your anti-pattern behaviors keep you stuck in your job and in cycles of finishing projects that don't quite get the results you were hoping for.

Once you understand your anti-patterns, you will then move on in Chapter 3 to learn how your biology fuels your decisions to follow those behaviors. While at first glance it may seem as if you're doomed—*My biological makeup is behind my failure to get a promotion? Is it really all my parents' fault?*—but you're not. Because, as you'll see in Chapter 4, which starts Part 2, you can learn how to take control of your biology and turn your anti-patterns into impactful actions.

You'll learn to create a strong foundation in Chapter 5 so when you build your Playbook, it's on solid emotional ground. Then, because many of our actions are reactions to things you didn't plan for, Chapter 6 will offer an alternative to reacting negatively to unpleasant events so that you can avoid hitting potholes on your way to making impact.

At that point, you'll be ready to create your own Impactful Actions Playbook and Part 3 dives into the details on how to do just that.

THE PLAN'S ORIGINS

One of the benefits of losing my standing with the making-impact club was that I got a beautiful view of things from the cheap seats, or as they say, I discovered hindsight really is 20/20.

Growing up, I was obsessed with the idea of being a video game developer. I spent every minute outside of school or sports obsessing over the details and nuances of what I had to do to become one. My teachers even thought I was a huge pain in the ass because I'd constantly remind them that their coursework wasn't helping me with my goal.

When I finally made it into the industry, I was primed for action, and in some cases, I rose in the ranks rather quickly. Until my ego started writing checks my compiler skills couldn't cash. I was quickly labeled a "difficult employee" and soon it didn't matter how valuable my code was, I was on the outs. I bounced around a bit before pivoting my career to developer education and training. Then with all the fury to prove I wasn't a one-trick-pony, I quickly started obsessing in that space too. Once again, I rose through the ranks. Until once again, my mouth and unchecked opinions got me into trouble. You'd think I'd have seen the pattern at that point, but no, I repeated it a third time, searching around, pivoting, and screwing up.

It wasn't until that third time that things finally sank in. Maybe it was age, maybe it was fatigue at the intensity of it all, or maybe it was some background pattern matching that my brain was doing. Whatever it was, it made me take a step back and say, "Whoa, I've got some problems I need to fix." I took some time and really dug into where I had been messing up. I laughed at my stupidity, cursed at my screwups, and overall, tried to see what worked and what didn't.

What became clear, was that my successes were almost always driven by a clear goal and a passion to be great at it. Both of which are good things when you want to make impact. But opposing that was what was fueling my failures, which had something to do with my ego, lack of emotional control, the tendency to focus on the wrong objectives, and to be frank, the audacity to mouth off at my bosses. The truth was clear: when I had a vision, a plan, and energy, there were very few things I couldn't accomplish. But once that impact started to taper off, all that excess emotional energy would get redirected into negative places where it would cloud my judgment, hurt my work relationships, and keep me from seeing my way out of the fog.

So that's where this process and planning started. It's from the realization of the connection between my emotional state and my ability to make traction on goals became clear to me. I didn't quite understand the mechanics at that time, but I knew if I were to break this wheel, to stop the cyclical pattern of working hard to get nothing done only to work hard some more, I needed to find a way to ensure my vision was never clouded over by the emotional steam.

But just because you can look out from a mountain vista and see a beautiful beach in the distance doesn't mean you are going to cut through the jungle growth filling the space between you and the ocean with ease. Clear vision is only one of the tools for making impact. I knew I'd need a plan, too. Some kind of roadmap or formula for not only recognizing what I needed to achieve but how to get there with the least amount of energy *and* without creating negative consequences.

I wanted to get back in the making-impact club and stay there. I wanted to figure out how to choose the right goals so that I'd find the right path to create the right impact only to do it all over again with bigger and better goals.

So I set out to become a "student of impact." At first, I was intent on learning as much as I could about how to make impact in my own life. But the further I went in my education, the more convinced I became that I needed to teach others how to do so as well. Coincidentally, the way I began the process has become one of the first things I teach people to do when they want to take action to make impact: observe the folks who are doing what you want to do.

Any time you're researching, if you begin by observing humans and absorbing their prior research, you'll be rewarded with early direction that helps you shape your events later. And that is exactly what happened to me. It didn't take long for me to notice enough shared habits of thought, patterns of behavior, and other characteristics for me to create a formula for making impact based on my observations.

The formula starts with understanding your true goals, which is followed by an evaluation of the skills you have at your disposal to achieve those goals. Then you can decide which actions you can take that would optimize the ratio between the results you want and the consequences you don't want.

It's a simple formula that creates an astounding impact. And it was one that explained my entrance, exit from, and readmittance to the making-impact club. The formula was something I'd internalized my whole life but hadn't quite put into words before.

BECOME A STUDENT OF IMPACT

Through this book, I hope you too become a student of impact. But beware, you will never graduate. Becoming a student of impact requires you to be in a constant study of yourself and the world around you. I can attest to this personally; you will need to be in a perpetual state of self-discovery and be willing to take responsibility for your actions. It's worth it, though. You will be rewarded with living a life that is ever broadening and ever-more fulfilling both professionally and even personally.

Fortunately, to take the first step to become a student of impact, you don't need any tools other than this book. You can get started when you turn the page and begin Part 1: Discover What's Blocking You from Making Impact, where we begin by talking about our goals. Because if you're not making impact, it's probably a safe bet to say that you're not achieving the kind of goals you need to achieve.

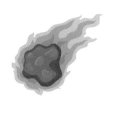

PART I

DISCOVER WHAT'S BLOCKING YOU FROM MAKING IMPACT

CHAPTER 1

THE ART OF GOAL SETTING

Whether it's landing a promotion, hitting a physical fitness target, or finally learning how to crochet a tracksuit, *something* has prevented you from reaching your goal. While this book is promising a solution to eliminate that something, before we can go there and do that, we need to lay some basic groundwork, which includes a discussion about goals.

A simple definition of *goal* from the dictionary is: "the object of a person's ambition or effort; an aim or desired result." While that's a fine, general, all-purpose definition, it's not quite effective for our means here. So let's back up a bit and ask, "Where do goals come from?" And maybe even add, "How do they serve us?" To answer those questions, let's talk about our low- and high-level goals.

LOW-LEVEL GOALS

As a living, breathing organism, you have a set of basic needs that must be met for your goal of staying alive. Breathing is one of them. Blood cells making a full circuit through your body is another. You don't have the option of controlling whether those goals are met. However, you can still impact them through behavior choices. Smoking, for instance, can make it difficult to breathe. Building cholesterol by overindulging in fast food, can set up blockages that can interfere with the smooth flow of blood coursing through your veins.

Similarly, and also biologically, there are certain goals you're programmed to pursue for which you really have no other choice but to accept the mission. Things like eating, mating, social bonding, and hoarding resources all fall under that rubric. They are more evolutionary in nature, having been assigned to our species to protect and ensure our existence. With these goals, again, our behavioral choices will determine how we make impact on them, but they remain goals regardless of whether we want them to be or not.

We're bringing up these biological goals here to open the discussion about how we are hardwired to care about our basic needs for survival. At the chemical level of our bodies, we're preprogrammed to ensure those goals are met, whether we want them to be or not. Take mating, for example. It may not be a goal for some individuals, but it is a necessary goal for the survival of the species. Many people are programmed with the desire to mate even though it is a rather inconvenient goal in many ways. It takes a huge amount of time and effort to raise offspring, yet we're driven to it so much that even those with the inability to do so, still adopt and raise children (which is awesome, those kids need good homes). Even with these hurdles, each species does it.

These low-level goals are so important to our survival that they are a priority for our body. We strive to meet them first and until they are met, all our other decisions are influenced by their lack. And when we cannot meet them, we instinctively scope different goals to fix those deficiencies, though, usually, we get poor results and leave collateral damage in our wake when we do so. Ever meet someone with a chip on their shoulder who is constantly out to prove themselves, doing so to the detriment of the others around them? Often their behavior is driven by the need to fill a deficiency in some low-level area. They are not able to engage in higher-order goal setting until they fulfill the deficiency.

You can think of it this way: At a biological level, your body is trying to meet these low-level goals. If they aren't met, then they bubble up into the rest of your mental processing, which means you now spend most of your time addressing them. Once they are met, however, your higher-order thinking is now opened to pursue other goals. Where we get into trouble is when those two things overlap without our understanding. For example, if you don't feel safe in your personal life, many decisions in your work life might be made to minimize coworkers stealing your lunch.

Spoiler alert: In Chapter 4 we're going to get to the bottom of how our biological chemicals influence our behavior at work and play throughout our entire lives. For now, though, just be aware that biologically, there are things you're working with that are driving your behavior and impacting your ability to achieve goals. How well those things are working and how easily those basic goals are met has an impact on all your higher-level goals.

HIGH-LEVEL GOALS

Once your low-level goals are met, you can start spending resources on discretionary needs. Those are things that may or may not support your basic needs but, regardless, are nice to have. For example, spending time picking wild berries will fulfill your need to alleviate hunger. However, a seven-course meal prepared by a Michelin-starred chef will too, and you'll probably enjoy it even more. Add in a few of your favorite people to enjoy the meal with and you're supporting the need for social belonging while having fun.

A good way to think about how high-level goals build on

top of our low-level ones is by using Maslow's hierarchy of needs. At the bottom of his hierarchy, we find the needs for air, water, food, shelter, sleep, clothing, and reproduction, which fuel our low-level goals. The further up this hierarchy you go, the more you'll find your higher-level goals are made possible because the ones in each preceding lower level were met. Perhaps ironically, we'll read from the top down what Maslow presents from the bottom up of his hierarchy of needs to see how the behaviors we choose depend on the level of goals we've already met.

- Basic survival needs (air, water, food, shelter, sleep, clothing, and reproduction) all drive our behavior through primal, biological processes to fulfill those goals.
- Safety needs, then, are able to be met with choices about personal security, employment, healthy lifestyles, and your home environment.
- Love and belonging goals can be our focus once we feel secure. We meet them with friendships, intimate relationships, family) and a sense of connection to others of like minds (e.g., game room chats).
- Esteem needs are next. Meeting them is possible only when we feel secure. Our goals at this level are fulfilled by choosing behaviors that build respect, self-esteem, assure some kind of status or recognition from others, and establish a sense of freedom over our choices.
- Self-actualization, at the top of Maslow's hierarchy, is

only possible when all the preceding needs are met. Here, we set goals with the desire to become the most that we can be.

By looking at your goals through the lens of Maslow's hierarchy, you can see the level that would best serve your needs to focus on. If you've just lost your job (a safety need), perhaps now is not the time to join a gym so you can meet more like-minded people (a belonging need). In other words, you can use the process of goal setting—viewed through Maslow's hierarchy—as a heuristic for prioritization.

FROM A BUSINESS PERSPECTIVE

From a business or work perspective, goals can be seen in the same way. Businesses, teams, sub-units, etc., all have a set of basic needs that must be met. Similar to humans, if a business doesn't meet its basic needs and its core goals, it perishes. Basic needs for a business include:

- Adequate revenue streams to keep the lights on and pay employees
- A minimum number of staff with appropriate skill sets to create the products or provide the services of the company
- A facility and equipment capable of fulfilling the company's reason for being, whether that's manufacturing

unique flavors of bubble gum or providing catering on demand
- Similar to the above: sourced vendors or suppliers necessary for fulfilling the company's reason for being

The higher-level goals for a business, the ones that come after meeting the basic needs are labeled "growth" goals. They are all about making the business more successful and include, among other ideas:

- Marketing targets for expanding the customer base
- Research and development for new or improved product or service ideas (perhaps unique flavors of jawbreakers to go along with the bubble gum)
- Employee training and skill set expansion
- Development of fun customer experiences to encourage brand loyalty

A key concept to understand with business goals revolves around failure. As with humans, if a company should fail to meet a basic goal, the company dies. But if it fails to meet a growth goal, it's called a missed opportunity.

Missing opportunity means impact wasn't made, which brings us back to the point of this book. Making impact means you're hitting goals—not just any goals, the right goals. And now that you know where goals come from, let's look at ways you can tell a goal is not the right one.

BAD GOALS DESERVE A BAD RAP

At first glance, it might seem impossible to have a bad or wrong goal. After all, we're driven by uncontrollable biological processes to meet our needs and we know what those needs are, so setting the right goals should be obvious. The keyword there is *should*. But again, if you're reading this book, then you know it's not always the case.

We just discussed how setting goals can be an act of prioritizing needs. To expand on that here, within each need there are often several potential avenues you can proceed to try to fulfill it. Many of those avenues are so cluttered with unnecessary information and ideas, though, that you risk scattering your attention unless you are clear about what you are doing and what you are going after. And therein lies the rub.

Often, when we choose a bad or wrong goal, we lack that clarity due to one of two reasons: We either do not know the truth about ourselves, or we do not know the truth about our goals. And since the only time it's healthy to keep secrets is when you're planning a surprise party, let's expose those truths by learning about bad goals caused by either a lack of self-awareness or falsehoods about the goal itself.

KNOW THYSELF

You are the first source of bad goals. We'll bring that up

several times in this book, so you may want to get used to that idea. And while that may sound like bad news, if you flip that concept around, you'll realize you are also the first source of good goals, which is quite empowering. Choosing good goals is a matter of developing self-awareness.

The self-awareness that is critical for making impactful decisions requires you to know what drives you and how to express it.

You're at the Wheel

Given that you have biological hardware nudging your decisions toward fulfilling a specific set of basic needs, you have to realize that you're not always in control of your goal setting. Those basic needs also lead to unconscious biases that influence how you choose your behaviors. Then, that lack of awareness leads to less optimal outcomes. You will constantly spend time and effort in areas that might serve core needs but likely will not result in any real progress. Let's say you're invited out for a beer after work on Friday. It's been a hard week for everyone, especially you, because you've been hunkered down almost in isolation working on the final bit of programming for a big launch. Without thinking, you immediately agree—unconsciously you're satisfying your need for social belonging. However, these friends have expensive tastes and, as often happens when you go out with them, you regret it the next day. Not because of the headache (well, maybe partly because of the headache), but because you should be saving money to buy a new and desperately needed car. In this case, serving the core need of belonging overtook your rational brain's idea of saving money.

We're not going to spend much time discussing this concept of taking control of your behaviors here, as it is the primary focus in the next chapter. So consider this a heads-up—getting to know yourself is what puts you in the driver's seat to make impact.

Communication Divergence

Part of knowing yourself is having a deep and thorough understanding of what you mean when you speak. That is, you make sure that your "mouth sounds" are properly communicating what your brain is thinking and that people listening get the right message. Failing to do so is a big risk: if your stated goal and actual goal diverge—that is, what you say and what you actually need are standing in two different lines at the Communication Fairgrounds—then any action you take toward your goals will result in a failure to make impact.

Let's say you want to get a promotion. So you make that your goal. But then your team has a project that needs to be completed. You're really passionate about that project, so you convince your manager you need to have an active role with it. Sure, you're acting like a great team member, but maybe you shouldn't be surprised if your manager denies you a promotion. Because while, in your mind, you are thinking this is what will get you promoted, in your words and actions you were communicating your excitement about the project. On top of that, your manager, although appreciating your efforts for the team, is still expecting you to make impact on the target she had set for you, which you subsequently didn't have time to work on.

Now then, *maybe* if you had mentioned to your manager that you hoped the project would count as your target for impact, they would have been able to tell you whether it would serve your goals for promotion.

Decision makers fall into this trap when they neglect to survey themselves for internal biases. We see this when they preach about the need to cut costs but then they favor a vendor for its convenient method for reordering supplies even though that vendor's cost far exceeds the extra manpower required for another vendor. This is also why managers should never say, "*Do whatever needs to be done to land this deal!*" unless they really are okay with the keys to their personal Porsche being thrown into the mix.

The single biggest problem in communication is the illusion that it has taken place.

—GEORGE BERNARD SHAW

The point here is that thinking about your goal and communicating your goal are two different skills. Taking the time to ensure your goals are clear to yourself and to anyone involved with you attaining them requires that you talk to yourself and others clearly and honestly about your goals. And that means you need to know your goals.

While it might seem like common sense that you need to know what your goal is, it's actually the second reason why people often choose bad or wrong goals: they don't know what their true goals are.

KNOW THY GOALS

Saying the phrase, *we do not know the truth about our goals* almost suggests there's some great mystery behind getting what we want, as if finding them would require us to travel down some magical golden road that takes us through scary apple-tree forests where we meet and make friends with quirky characters and fight off witches until we get to a magical castle where all the answers can be found. But that's something for a different book.

Here, there is no mystery. In fact, the rest of this chapter is devoted to learning the difference between bad or wrong goals and good goals. Once you can feel confident in making a good goal, you will be able to set a course of action to achieve it. You know, make impact.

So let's discuss how to know whether you have a good goal.

What Is Your Goal? Can You Answer that Question Clearly?

When Harry Potter stepped onto platform 9¾, he had one goal: become a wizard. That was it. He was willing to follow any giant, battle any dragon, or carry any owl, as long as he could call himself a wizard someday. While a fine premise for an adventure, that's a bad goal, simply because it's too vague. Vague goals run into problems of not being concrete enough to be achievable. Or they are so broad, that achieving them doesn't really mean much. Our wizarding friend had a lot of help in his path to achieve his goal but unless you've got access to a magic wand store, vague goals can lead you astray.

If you're not really clear where you are heading, you won't know if you're on the right road and, worse, you may not know if you ever arrive. Fortunately, vague goals are easily identified. All you have to do is ask, *what's the next step?* If no clear action step reveals itself, then you have a vague goal. That's the difference between *I want to be famous* and *I want to be a famous singer on Broadway before age thirty-*

five. The first one doesn't provide any clues about how to become famous. The second, meanwhile, lets you know you need to acquire singing, dancing, and acting lessons, not to mention a penchant for overdone makeup.

At work, where our impact is measured based on our goals, things can get tricky when we're given a vague goal. When that happens, we are forced to redefine and refine such vague goals in order to know how to take initiative.

Goals such as "We need to improve user happiness," are vague. How do you measure user happiness? You'll probably never get special permission to tap into your user's brains to measure dopamine release, so you'll need to create something else to measure what would signify an increase in their pleasure. We refer to the act of creating proxy metrics for things we can't directly measure, as *operationalization*. It's a word that might impress your lead when you tell her you're going to operationalize the team's happiness goal by measuring the increase in clicks on a webpage. And setting that user-clicks goal will give you the action steps to take to proceed.

Once you know your goal well enough that you can define your goal and see steps to take toward it, the next thing to do is to stack the deck to make taking those steps—that is, go into action—as easy as possible. That brings us to the second question to ask to discern whether or not you have a good goal.

Are You Set Up to Achieve Your Goal?

Taking action to achieve a goal requires you to take an assessment of your life to see how you will fit your actions toward your goal into it. That includes evaluating:

- Your access to resources,
- Your ability to make room in your life for the actions required of you, and
- Your perspective of your goal.

What Resources Do You Have?

Resources are always required to reach a goal. Whether it's making lunch or bringing in an extra $1 billion for the company, you have to leverage time, money, raw materials, approvals, and other people to make it happen. Not understanding what it takes to achieve your goal will put you in a risky position.

There are a variety of ways misunderstanding your resources can bite you. One is from the problem just mentioned: If your goal is vague, you won't know what resources are necessary to achieve it. But problems can still arise when you completely understand your goal—sometimes the resources you need simply aren't available to you. They might not exist at all, or you might lack the skills to gain access to them on behalf of your goal.

Goals with limited or nonexistent resources are often the result of poor planning. Not thinking through the actual amount of time it takes to do a task or expecting income from a revenue stream that wasn't properly vetted, can lead to an unintentional lack of time and money. While poor planning is never an optimal approach to your goals—and is something you'll abandon once you learn the playbook later—even worse is setting a goal for which you knowingly, blatantly, lack the resources to achieve. Yet people do this— all the time. It's the old "if you shoot for the moon and miss, you still end up in the stars" philosophy that some folks like to bat around big-picture ideas. They'll set huge goals that are impossible to achieve, thinking they are motivating themselves or others, as if certain failure is inspirational.

Associated with not understanding the resources required for your goal is the tendency to artificially restrict your goals. We've all seen this play out countless times in brainstorming meetings. Someone will be kicking one idea after another to the curb without doing due diligence to see what's available to them. Or they lock into a decision based on a false premise. Narrowing your options without due diligence is what all of those *think-outside-the-box* posters in the office are trying to help you avoid.

As you're picking goals, making decisions, or deciding actions, you want to open yourself up to the broadest options possible, which requires you to think about it from a different perspective. Maybe you aren't as resource constrained as you thought. Maybe you can get the same effect but with a different angle. Or maybe you were wrong about what the VP was asking you to do all along.

Do Your Resources and Actions Fit into Your Life?

Whatever your resources are, whatever actions they lead you to take, you have to pre-plan how they will fit into your life. Many New Year's resolutions are broken due to failing to do just that. How many times have you or someone you know announced that *this* is the year he was going to get a grip on his work-life balance and yet, sometime around January 24th, they're working fourteen-hour days and can't remember their kids' names?

Here, the unknowns are what muddies the waters of achieving goals. It can be difficult to figure out how to fit the required changes into your life if you don't know what they are. Sure, you might say you'll just set a timer to pack up at 4:55 p.m. everyday so you're out the door by five o'clock. But if you don't change your work habits, like learning to prioritize tasks or mastering how to say no while at work, how will that even be possible?

In some cases, the goal you want to achieve isn't possible simply because you lack the emotional foundation to achieve it. Maybe you haven't mastered the self-discipline possible to wake up in the morning. Or you don't have the experience needed to speak confidently to VPs. While having a goal can force you to grow these kinds of skills, you should be aptly aware that without the right foundation, achieving your goals will be significantly more difficult. So not only do you need to make room in your schedule, your lifestyle, and your work habits, but you need to make room in your emotional foundation to grow such skills.

Are You Looking at Bling or the Real Deal?

It's a very dangerous situation to romanticize a goal. So much so that we find warnings about it in stories throughout human history. In epic tales and moralistic movies, we find someone has a big goal that they strive for above all else, but they end up losing their family, alienating their friends, and destroying everything around them to get it. Similar are the stories of someone pining after a crush, only to realize later that their dream partner is exceptionally boring or self-centered.

A more modern equivalent is one we see at work in people who aim to be on "the perfect team," the one with the amazing track record. They expect their career to rocket up from it, but once on the team, they discover a group of horrible people, demanding too much of their life in general.

At its core, our excitement about one aspect of our goals can blind us to the realities of the other aspects. If we let ourselves get caught in such reckless obsession, we've ventured into pursuing a destructive goal. The only avoidance of this is to make sure you've done the research so that you know the good and the bad of what you're trying to achieve.

Actually, you may have noticed a pattern among these questions—they each require an element of research to properly answer. And that is what is at the core of knowing your goal.

WHAT IT ALL COMES DOWN TO

At the end of the day, these bad goals share a common thread: They are built out of a lack of research and a poor understanding about yourself and your business. The more ignorant you are about these factors, the worse your goals are and the less impactful you become, which makes learning how to pick a good goal imperative.

GET SOME CONTEXT: STORYTIME WITH COLT

Lisa was troubled by the protests against racial injustice that had been happening across the country. She wanted to do something about them but had no idea what or if anything she could do would actually be of benefit to anyone. A friend of a friend introduced her to me and asked if I could help her.

"I feel so helpless right now," she said to me. "I want to help."

"Could you volunteer at a soup kitchen?" I asked. I wasn't trying to be flippant, nor was I being obtuse. She didn't know me well and had seemed hesitant to talk to me. One of the things I'd learned as a mentor is that by asking someone something audacious, they would often open up to make themselves more clear. So I had intentionally asked the sideways question.

"I mean, I could," she said, "but how does that help with the protests?"

"Oh, the protests! Have you been participating in them?"

"No," she replied sheepishly. "I'm not a hero. The thought of getting caught between police and looters keeps me from going down there."

"I see. So you want to help with that situation somehow, right?"

"Yeah."

"As in create some kind of civil change?"

"Well, yes," she sighed. "But that feels too big for me alone.

I mean, besides arguing and voting, I'm not sure what else I can do."

"Well, before we get to what you can do, let's unpack what you're going through. You don't feel comfortable protesting and you are somewhat limited in your ability to create civil change. You know that and you've accepted that. So what is happening that's causing you stress?"

That question was an important one because it encouraged Lisa to stop considering what she could do to help the overall situation and focus on what about that situation hit closest to home. That is, it helped refine her goal to be less vague. And it worked. She didn't hesitate to answer.

"The cops," she said. "The police brutality is horrible. There's no reason for that type of behavior. These people are trying to make civil change, to make things better, and they're getting arrested and ending up in the hospital. One of my friends has a $40,000 doctor bill from being assaulted by police officers during a protest. He doesn't have that kind of money."

Her answer clarified for both of us what was at her core that was driving her toward taking action.

"Wow, that's really bad," I said. "I'm so sorry to hear that.

But it gives me an idea. What if we focused on helping the people who went down to peacefully protest but might have been arrested or injured while doing so?"

"Yes!" she said, her energy level rising.

But I wasn't done. We needed to do more than just elevate her mood. She needed a plan of action if she was going to make impact on her goal to help.

"So what do these folks need?" I asked. "They've been arrested or they've ended up in the ER. How can we help with that?"

"I don't know. Maybe bail them out? Or maybe I could take them to the hospital?"

"Okay, that's a start. But bailing them out costs money; can you afford that?"

She shook her head.

"And driving them to the ER requires your presence at the protests, which we've already ruled out. So let's do some research here." Because her idea reflected that she didn't have the resources available to her (funds or willingness to be at the protests), we had to get more clarity. I gave her some homework to find out what was already going on. Who was currently involved in helping the protestors. What systems were already in place?

About an hour later, Lisa returned with quite a bit of information.

"I found a bunch of lawyers who will represent these people pro bono. And I found a few 501(c)3 charities who will provide them with money for expenses. So it seems like they are already taken care of."

It was clear she was disappointed and veering toward feeling helpless again. Likewise, it was clear she had narrowed down her options too far. "How hard was it for you to find all that data?" I asked.

"Well, I had to comb through a bunch of social media sites and asked a bunch of people."

"Do you think a random person protesting would be able to do that? Do they know your friends?"

"No."

"So it seems like you're in a unique position. You've got information that can help the protesters find assistance when they need it. How can you get this information to the people?"

That was the magic question! Lisa bubbled over with enthusiasm and ideas. "We could make an app for people to get this information. But apps are too hard to get...plus you don't want to have your cellphone with you all the time. Hmmm...what if we made a website. People could go to it and find lawyers and charities in case they need help."

"Perfect! That's a great goal. But now let's clarify it some more so we can figure out action steps. So we need a website. How fast can you build one?" Asking these questions helped set her up to take action.

"Oh, I'm not an engineer," she said, chewing her lip. "And I don't think I could really pay anyone to do that." Her constraints of time and resources were holding her back again. But instead of letting her worry about restrictions, I redirected her.

"What about your friend network? Do you know any web designers? Or anyone who might know someone? You could reach out to ask and let them know it would need to be pro bono and that it's to help people who really need it."

"Ooooh! That might work! My friend Casey is a designer for a big tech company."

Once again I gave her some homework and we promised to speak the next day. The homework was a necessary break so that she could ruminate on the idea some more and explore more potential avenues to get things done. To help her stay on track with the process, I set a few goals for her:

Reach out to her friends with an email or DM to see who would be willing to give six to eight hours of time to help get a website online.

Contact the lawyers and the 501(c)3 groups, tell them what she's trying to do, and ask their permission to list their contact information.

I gave her a script of what to say so that she wouldn't be afraid to make the connections, and she was off.

The next day, Lisa came in, bouncing off the walls. During the night she had spoken with her friends and they were eager to help. Within a few hours, a website was up, the domain was purchased with unexpected donations, and everything was up and running. Feeling confident, she reached out to more places and her friends were finding new ones to include.

"We're doing two things," she said. "First, we have resources to help people protest safely and understand how to keep safe in that situation. We also made cards that they can print, tape, and keep on them so they can call the lawyers if they need to. Also, someone called us back and gave us a phone number that people can Sharpie on their arms because their phones will be taken if they go to jail. Then, for those people, we have resources to help."

While we were speaking she received a phone call from one of the lawyers she had contacted.

"OMG!" she shouted when she hung up. 'They're sharing our information on Twitter!"

When I had given her the homework to contact attorneys and nonprofits that could help, I told her it was to ask them for permission to use their contact info on the website. But really, it was for her to create allies and expand her resource pool for future projects. Most of the firms want clients, so they need free marketing, which Lisa's site was providing. If everything was successful, it would be a win-win situation that required us to know what other resources we have by understanding the needs of the people around us.

This is an example of helping someone refine their goal. Lisa was in a bad spot because she had artificially constrained herself, thinking there was only one type of action for her to take. By continuing to ask questions, helping her think about different ways to see her options, we opened up more goals and, in the end, found what she was looking for.

HOW TO CHOOSE A GOOD GOAL

Now that you're armed with the ability to recognize a bad goal, it will be easier to see a good one standing in front of you; it will have the opposite characteristics. When you have a good goal, you:

- Can clearly define it and recognize action steps to get started
- Have effective resources available to achieve it
- Have an open path to it, where you are not restricted in some way that would prevent you from going after it
- Have a full perspective and are not only going after the pretty, shiny parts
- Have figured out how to fit it into your life

But there's a little more to good goals. We need to tweak our definition of them just a tad more to ensure they are the right ones for us. Here are a few more things to consider.

ARE YOUR BASIC NEEDS MET?

As mentioned earlier, if your basic goals aren't met, that's where you need to start—by fixing any deficiencies there. Otherwise, you risk setting goals with a skewed perspective of what you need to do. When you make a goal, you are choosing where to direct your efforts and which stimuli you respond to. If you have a deficiency and your goals aren't toward remedying that deficiency first, then you are going to be less impactful overall. The deficiency will seep into everything you do. Little bits of energy and attention and mis- resourced time will turn into trying to fulfill the deficiency rather than what you're working on. For you to be impactful, you have to clear your plate and make things right first.

Taking care of your basic needs first is a rule that applies to yourself and your work. If you're a team lead, are you meeting the basic requirements of your team's existence? Are you keeping your stakeholders happy and contributing to their end goals? If not, you will not have the energy, time, or space to take on discretionary tasks because you'll risk being defunded or disbanded.

So if you have a plan at work to create a new process to fix a production problem, that's great. But if the problem is really because the coworkers on that line don't get along, then the new process is most likely going to make things worse because that dysfunctional team will now need to learn a new process together.

HAVE YOU DONE YOUR RESEARCH?

You knew this section was coming. In all the problems with bad goals, we mentioned research as a remedy. It just makes sense to do it. The more data you have, the more enabled you will be to make informed decisions. Besides, researching what goes into a good goal can be kind of fun. Try these methods:

- Project yourself into success. Yes, you do need to "be careful what you wish for," but if you spend some time visualizing yourself in the desired place you want to be, you'll be sparked with insight to help you make it a clearly defined goal with actionable steps.
- Ask someone who's been where you want to be. We'll discuss this further in the Playbook, but interviewing people to discover what it's really like to have achieved a goal and what it took to get there can be quite helpful.
- Look at your goals from several perspectives. You might realize that your goal isn't sound or that there's a better subgoal to accomplish first. Or it could be that it's blocked by something that needs to be opened for you, perhaps there's a limit to how many people can be on the team you're aiming for so you need to wait for someone to leave and make a vacancy for you, or maybe the store is sold out of pickled mango ice cream so you can't make your favorite sundae for dessert.
- Get a good sounding board. By articulating your needs to someone else, you can get good feedback. This can help ensure you are aligning your real goals with your stated goals and give you an opportunity for an honest gut check to determine you're heading in the right direction.
- Refine your goal as best you can. Try and keep it as

simple as possible, as specific as possible, and keep it loose. We'll discuss this loose concept later, but here, "loose" means it's important to understand that you need to be open to how you achieve your goals. In some cases, your goal will define the action steps for getting there, but often you'll be presented with opportunities to do something different that may be more beneficial. Be open to those different paths.

WHAT IF IT'S NOT YOUR GOAL?

It's much easier to define and go after a goal you've set for yourself, but so many times in our lives, we're given our goals. Whether it's from parents or family members, teachers, professors, people at work, or the government, there will always be a stakeholder telling us "Hey! You gotta do this." In effect, they're setting goals for us and expecting us to make impact for them. In such cases, all the above ideas hold true. You will also build your Playbook for these kinds of goals the same way you will for your personal goals.

The clever trick here is to always turn their goal into your goal. You have to figure out how to make it valuable to you. This is something I frequently discuss with managers when they're tasked with something they aren't passionate about. By trying to follow through without taking ownership of the goal, or not connecting it to some personal context, they risk spiraling into depression. Stopping that spiral requires seeing how the task still benefits their own personal, larger goals. For example, most of us have an end goal to have money, right? Then this shitty job helps with that. Or your goal might be to pad your résumé for the next job, in which case we can rewrite this shitty task as something to help with that.

PUTTING IT ALL TOGETHER

From both a hardware and software level, your body is driven to achieve goals. At a physical level, there are goals so important that your body will bias all your higher-order thinking until they are achieved. Only at the point when they are met can your brain open up more energy for the next level of goal setting. The basics of food, water, and shelter then lead into social acceptance and self-worth, which are further up the pyramid of realization. Understanding that these goals are gated on one another is critical. Only once we recognize and address those needs can we start opening ourselves up to higher-level goal setting and planning.

But even then, we have to be aware that there is trouble brewing. It's critical to understand that picking shortsighted, mis-resourced, biased goals, means that you're setting yourself up for failure before you even start. One could argue that inability to recognize good and bad goals is one of the most self-destructive behaviors you can have in a professional setting.

Likewise, we have to understand that in our work lives, we're constantly being given goals that others task us to achieve. While we can't always control their decision-making and (good or bad) goal selection, we can elevate ourselves above, making sure that we're making progress on our own goals while working on others.

So congratulate yourself for knowing you have goals, and you want to achieve them. Achieving them depends on the actions you take to do so—more specifically on whether those actions are impactful or unimpactful. Because it's important to unravel those before you can make a Playbook to achieve your goals, we'll next discuss how to identify unimpactful actions.

CHAPTER 2

UNIMPACTFUL ACTIONS

Now that you have a good goal, you may be ready to make a run for it, take action, and achieve it. But although you might be on the mark and set, you're not quite ready to go just yet. Remember learning about the interspecies marathon between the hare and the tortoise? The hare has energy. It has drive. It has the ability to get where it wants to go. But the tortoise winds up standing at the finish line with the winning medal around her neck. Do you know why that upset happened?

If you answered with "because the hare took a nap," you get partial points. It happened because the tortoise took *impactful* actions to make steady progress toward her goal of winning the race. Meanwhile, the hare took an *un*impactful action, that infamous nap, and while, yes, he was able to cross the finish line without being winded, that wasn't his goal. He looked good in gold. He wanted that medal.

In short: *Impactful actions are actions we take that ultimately lead to our goal.* Unimpactful actions are actions we take that lead to everywhere else. The hare's nap led her to second place.

The tricky thing is, sometimes an action that is impactful toward one goal is unimpactful for others. That infamous nap we just mentioned, for example. A nap can be an impactful action. It just depends on the situation you might find yourself in. Artist Salvador Dali and scientist Albert Einstein are famous nappers, and their power naps were impactful actions. Why? Their naps helped them think clearly, find solutions, and figure things out. And that's what impactful actions are all about: clear thinking, solutions, and determining ways to make those solutions happen.

NAP LIKE DALI

Speaking of naps, fun fact. The Surrealist artist didn't nod off to the point of snoring. His napping style made great use of something called hypnagogia: that state between sleep and being awake. In his *50 Secrets of Magic Craftsmanship,* he claims that, that briefest of time spent being almost asleep is enough and "not a second more is needed for your physical and psychic being to be revivified." To nap like Dali, do his "Slumber with a key" method. Set a plate upside down on the floor beside you, sit upright (preferably in a Spanish ebony chair), and hold a key in your hand (a plastic hotel magnetic one won't do, you'll need something metal). Close your eyes and let yourself fall asleep. The key will drop from your relaxed hand and clang on the plate, waking you up when naptime is over.

So unimpactful actions, then, are the opposite. Unimpactful actions do not contribute to achieving our goals. They hinder our progress because we have problems in one or more of the following three buckets:

1. Problems with our goals
2. Problems with the types of actions we take
3. Problems with our foundations

When we take action without fixing the problems in those buckets, that action rarely has the ability to make the kind of impact we want to make. But because the problem remains unfixed, we repeat that mistake and try to take action again with equally less than impressive results. *This is how we form anti-patterns, which is what we call it when we frequently repeat the same problematic behaviors.*

It's important to know what your anti-patterns are because you cannot make impactful actions until you understand why you're making unimpactful ones. So to that end, let's dive into the buckets.

PROBLEMS WITH OUR GOALS BUCKET

You just read an entire chapter about how to avoid bad goals and choose a good one, so we don't need to go there again. What we do need to talk about here, though, is how our goals can cause us to take *un*impactful actions.

- Vague goals reduce the impact of your actions. Let's say your team breaks for lunch. Everyone gets up and walks around until they find something. Vague goal? *Check.* Hungry group of coworkers who are getting increasingly grumpy? Also *check.* Any action taken toward a vague goal is more difficult since so much extra time and effort needs to be put toward refining that goal. If you don't have a clear path to get there, you can be certain you don't have a clearly defined goal and every action you then take will be unimpactful.

- By underestimating the resources required to reach a goal, your actions will always be stalled due to a lack of options. On the other side, if you've under-estimated your needs, then you might have boxed yourself in and not seen the breadth of actions you could have taken. Again, the wrong goal here has hurt your ability to make impact on it before you even started.

- If you get distracted and focus on only one exciting part of your goal, all your actions will be unimpactful because they will be toward the pretty and shiny thing and *not* to the whole of what you want. It won't matter how perfectly designed your spreadsheet is if you've been so busy working on it that you haven't been able to collect the customer data to go in it for the end project.

- If you are not set up to achieve your goals, there will not be room in your schedule, energy in your body, or space in your head for your actions. Your actions will be unimpactful because they will be limited if they can even happen at all.

While bad goals lead you astray, good goals can also be problematic by leading you to take unimpactful actions. Here's what to look for.

PERPETUALLY GUNNING FOR THE NEXT GOAL

It's relatively easy to convince yourself you're making impact when you are hitting one short-term goal after another on multiple fronts. However, if you find yourself doing that, maybe you should take a hard look at what you're really doing. Perhaps all that action you're expending on those short-term goals could be put to better use. If you are always looking for a new, quick, and easy goal to achieve, that might mean you're not quite tackling the big ones.

This book is being written during the COVID pandemic, an era where we all need small wins. For a lot of folks, just making a goal to wake up, get out of bed, and make breakfast is a huge win. And doing that reliably is a massive one. For individuals with PTSD due to emotional drama—ex-military, someone who's experienced a tragic, traumatic event, or a crime victim—small daily goals are important and valuable.

Sometimes we have to adopt a short-term goal framework. But the important thing is, even for individuals going through a tough time, there are always larger goals they're moving toward. They just have to create a ladder of sub-goals to get there. If the larger goal is to get back to being a functioning human on a regular basis, then the short-term sub-goal is just to cook eggs today without crying. And that's okay; Cook yourself some bad-ass eggs. Small goals have a necessity.

OUR ACTIONS ARE NOT IN ALIGNMENT WITH OUR WHY

As you take action toward a goal, whether it's a short-term or long-term one, you should always know the why behind your action. Asking some basic questions to get to the bottom of your why will often provide clarity around whether your actions will be impactful or unimpactful.

Asking *Why am I doing this? What will I gain from it?* or *Is it leading me to where I want to go?* and then answering honestly, might just reveal you're taking an action that won't get you what you think it will. Sure, organizing a bowling team among your group may encourage social bonding with them, but that doesn't necessarily mean you'll work better together in a professional setting. Perhaps a better use of that time and energy would be finding group training or task-related fun activities that would be more impactful in the long run.

He who has a why to live for can bear almost any how.

—FRIEDRICH NIETZSCHE

By questioning *why* not only will you get clarity on whether your actions are aligned with the right goals, but you will get clarity on what's really motivating you and whether that motivation is enough to maintain your drive to reach those goals.

Let's look at launching your own business. You may tell yourself you're doing it for the promise of a better income. While that is a fine reason to take action and launch it, unless you receive a substantial income, it may not motivate you to put in the sustained effort (i.e., sustained actions) required for the extra hours necessary to get your company beyond the start-up phase. So you have to ask yourself what will? And the answer to that is your true motivating factor for taking action. Is it freedom? You don't want to feel like you're beholden to another entity? Is it feeling respected for your talents? Is it because every day is bring-your-pet-ferret-to-work day?

By tapping into your motivation to do something, you

will find the gift of grit and determination to get the job done. But only if that motivation is set in a sound and healthy rationality.

OUR MOTIVATION HAS UNHEALTHY REASONS

One of the reasons that we sometimes don't make impactful actions relates to when our lower-level goals are not met. One way to know if you're in such a situation is when you look in the mirror and ask yourself why you are doing what you're doing, or why you want a particular goal and you get an answer that appeals to your baser instincts—vanity, ego, greed, lust, or evil. By taking action from that standpoint, you'll probably never find satisfaction. While those baser instincts are a function of your existence in this universe, nothing really valuable comes from them. Like empty calories, they fuel you with nothing good. Achieving goals in their honor will only lead to an emptiness inside you. Whereas achieving goals by taking actions motivated by healthier reasons will provide that satisfaction and happiness.

We all know pay raises often go hand-in-hand with promotions. So it's easy to fall into the trap of wanting a promotion just for the extra money. But if that's the only reason—to have more money—then ask yourself *why*. Is it because you think you're not being paid enough? If *yes*, then that's appealing to your baser instincts of greed. And you will never make "enough" money. But if your *why* is answered with a laundry list of what the money will give you, then you might find the roots of healthy motivation. If it will afford you the ability to make rent each month, then it's fulfilling a basic need. If it will be a means to allow you to go to school to better your education, then it's a good stepping-stone toward a long-term goal. Both those latter reasons for the promotion are healthy motivators in that they have lasting power and will make you feel good when you accomplish the goal. They are also strong enough to help sustain your energy and drive as you make impactful action.

GET SOME CONTEXT: STORYTIME WITH COLT

In a mentoring session, an individual I was working with lamented about his manager. He was so angry, he wanted to switch teams. He just couldn't stand anybody on his current team. He found them beyond frustrating and all he could do was talk and talk and vent and spew about them and the manager. His anger reached a boiling point and spilled over into the team meetings and into his personal relationships as well. He was so wound up in his rage, you couldn't have a talk with him without the negativity coming up. So we went through a process to break things apart to get to the core of his problems.

"What is feeding this anger?" I asked. "Do you have a manager who hits you with a stick?"

He gave me a side-eye.

"Did your team members tell you that you were not valuable?" I pressed on. "Did they harass you?"

"No," he said after a pause. "They just don't understand me."

"What do you mean?"

"Oh, you know, their goals are different than my goals, so I don't want to do the work that they have."

"Well, okay. But you're on a team and sometimes teamwork requires doing work you don't want to because that's how we get the job done. So why don't you want to do the work? And what does that have to do with them not understanding you?"

We went back and forth on this with me being persistent to get to a root cause of the dissatisfaction and anger. And it turned out that the reason he was upset was because the manager was giving him tasks that he felt were beneath him. And the reason he was upset with all of his peers was because they weren't coming to him asking for help. He felt the gravitas of his status was being ignored. He was an expert, after all, they should be coming to him for advice!

He was angry because he wasn't getting the validation for

his skills that his vanity felt he deserved. And this was creating a negative atmosphere everywhere else he went.

So I asked if he was willing to try an experiment. "I want to fix this," I told him. "But I'm worried you're too far gone. I'm worried that you've already damaged your relationships with your manager and your coworkers beyond repair. Quite frankly, you can either leave the team now, which is what it seems like you're trying to do. Or you can try to fix it."

I knew if he didn't try to fix it, he'd be at risk of taking his attitude and his problems with him, which would ensure he'd find himself in a similar situation with another team. But he wasn't in a position to hear that reasoning, so I had to leave the decision up to him.

He agreed to stay. It was the recession, after all, and it would be difficult to find someone hiring at his level.

It was obvious to me that if his goal really was to seek validation, then what was motivating him was vanity or ego; he was trying to fill a low-level goal of insecurity. I worked with him to create a framework that would help him feel more secure with his place in the world.

"Because you are an expert," I said, "maybe you could help the sales team. They go out on calls with very limited knowledge of the technical side of things. Perhaps you could help them when clients have questions."

He began participating on sales calls. The salespeople were delighted to have the support and the customers, who frequently didn't understand the value they offered at the level of depth he could explain, were beyond appreciative of his ability to help them figure out the solutions for their problems.

Everyone was happy, including the person I helped. His entire worldview changed. Instead of being upset with his manager, he didn't care what level of work his manager gave him. He happily complied because it was just part of the process, part of the goal of feeling secure with his place in the world. Likewise, he didn't seek validation from his coworkers.

At that point, I was frank with him. I said, "Okay, now let's take out the vanity completely and let's actually get you contributing back to other people."

We set him up as a mentor and a teacher for high school students and individuals from underrepresented areas who were looking to get into technology. By doing so, we gave him a chance to go out and find people who didn't understand their end goal and didn't know how to get there and let him show them the path. It was an empowering exercise for him. And when all the dust settled, he realized that the end goal for him wasn't about leaving his team. The end goal wasn't about the project the team was working on. But the end goal was that he wanted to feel a sense of purpose in his life.

PROBLEMS WITH OUR ACTIONS

The second bucket of problems that create anti-patterns of behavior involves our actions themselves. There are a variety of flavors with these problems. You can choose the wrong actions to take. You could spend too much time focusing on the execution of your actions or you can take actions that produce unintended results.

The key to taking the right action is to remember that *actions themselves are not valuable, but the impact they create is.* You can spend all day sharpening your favorite knife, but that doesn't mean your dinner will get cooked. But if you get the knife sharpened quickly enough that you can get the vegetables chopped in time to cook in a stew, then sharpening your knife was an impactful action. Otherwise, the excessive sharpening was unimpactful.

Here are other forms of unimpactful actions.

AGGRESSIVE INACTION

Aggressive inaction is when we refuse to take an action due to self-imposed mental traps that we create over fearing the consequences, particularly consequences leading to loss of some kind, from our actions. Being afraid of sunk costs or being loss or risk averse are often what lurks beneath aggressive inaction.

Not wanting to experience loss is a basic human fear. Setting aside teething babies and dieters who step on a scale only to discover it's gone up instead of down, it's commonly accepted that we're twice as sensitive to loss as we are to gain, which means we are more prone to protect ourselves against loss. With sunk costs, we're afraid to walk away from a potential loss because we don't want to feel the pain of admitting it's gone.

Fear of sunk costs will lead us to carry on with a failing project as we assert, "We can't do anything different. We've already put a million dollars into this project. We can't just cancel it now." The fear of sunk costs also explains why we remain in the theater seat even though we can't stand the movie at the midway point. We stick there through the end because we don't want the motherload of cash we put out to pay for the ticket and popcorn to go to waste. Interestingly, we don't stop to consider the value of our time.

Fun fact: Fear of sunk cost is very much tied to the fear of criticism. We've put time, effort, and resources into this, only to discover we're wrong. We don't often like admitting when we're wrong and certainly don't like when other people point it out. So we convince ourselves that pushing forward is more valuable than turning back. Don't let yourself believe in that false premise. Always remember that giving up on a bad goal is just as good as completing a good one. Set your ego aside and focus on your impact.

Fear of sunk costs creeps in *after* you've begun taking action, meanwhile being loss averse *may prevent* you from taking appropriate actions in the first place. When you are loss averse, you take the most conservative approach possible even though it has far less potential for benefit than a more daring one. Being loss averse can make us so hesitant to put effort into actions we fear will not be impactful, that we wind up taking no action. Being loss averse tells you to not apply for a dream job because you believe you're barely qualified to get it. It's also why you just can't make yourself ask someone you find amazingly attractive out on a date. We tell ourselves it's better to have the dream than to risk it being squashed.

Like being loss averse, being risk averse can also lead to inaction. Risk aversion tends to set in after we've taken some impactful actions that led to a comfortable level of success in a company or in life. We reach a point where we feel safe, so we stop playing to win and instead, we start playing *not* to lose. We get so good at avoiding anything we perceive as a risk that we fail to recognize the opportunities in front of us, training our focus on preserving the status quo and take little or no action.

Risky adventures with money, our emotions, or precious resources do need to be thought and planned to minimize the negatives as much as possible. But we need to be honest with ourselves about what those negatives are. Frequently, we'll insist that we're most worried about money or operational resources, but usually it's time we truly don't want to lose, or it's a matter of ego and the cognitive effort that could potentially be wasted in exchange for a damaged reputation. This is true even with something as trivial as walking out of a movie theater in the middle of a show. Is it really about the money you just spent? Or is it FOMO— the fear of missing out—on a potentially great ending "everybody else" will be talking about? Or possibly, is it the fear of discovering you're among the rare few who just don't "get it," and you're worried you'll look uncultured or uneducated?

You cannot make impact unless you break through your fear barriers to move beyond the analysis paralysis that aggressive inactions ultimately lead us to. Analysis paralysis happens when we're aware of our opportunities, but we can't take the right actions because we thought too long and too hard on the potential negatives. We end up sitting in a quagmire, spinning our wheels and never really do anything. (Facing your fears is something you'll be armed to do with the Playbook presented in Part II.

MULTITASKING

Let's all say this out loud: multitasking is a myth.

Sharing your attention is just bad. It makes you ineffective. Our brains simply cannot focus on more than one thing at a time. As you'll learn in the next chapter, there's a lot going on inside your skull that you're not even aware of. Expecting your cognitive abilities to bounce among a variety of projects with equal focus and attention is just asking too much.

The word "multitasking" is a bit of a misnomer, anyway. When you say you're multitasking, what you're really doing is task switching, which creates cognitive overhead. As your brain pops back and forth among projects, you accumulate more to manage: more task lists, more time schedules, more reminders, more emails, more calls, more whatever. It's a lot to keep up with, which is why many people in organizations get overwhelmed with the busy-ness of business. They're juggling several projects at the same time; each assignment requires a baseline effort, and a multitude of mini tasks get discretionary effort. All of that combined requires a considerable amount of voluntary attention, way beyond minimum effort.

When we constantly switch between too many things, we seldom make progress on any of them, which means we're not making progress with our goals. That lack of progress is what underlies vague actions, our next problematic action.

Vague Actions

Vague actions are what we do when we're working hard but aren't producing anything tangible in the real world. For example, someone might write down on her task list: *today I need to think about the plot for a novel*, or *I need to analyze the market options*. Both sound like actions but they're not really. They don't result in a manifestation of an artifact or a manifestation of anything in the physical world.

In contrast, drafting the plot outline of a novel in bullet points is not a vague action. You're producing a tangible product. Likewise, listing three sources of information about the market and contacting a source to get a feel for how particular industries are trending are not vague actions. You have to make the list, make the call or send an email—you have to generate something.

Concrete actions produce artifacts, while vague ones do not. If your action set is too vague then your actions will mostly take place in your head and not get you anywhere in the real world. Real-world actions, meanwhile—the right ones, anyway—are where you can make impact.

We tend to rely on vague actions because they make us feel as if we're doing something when, really, we're not. That sense of feeling is what brings us to our next problematic anti-pattern actions: Feel-good actions.

FEEL-GOOD ACTIONS

Sometimes it's amazing how prone humans are to taking actions that make us feel good, even though we get no traction with them. Take politics for example. We'll vent, rant, post on social media, and argue with our uncle over Thanksgiving dinner about politics, and none of that will change a damn thing. But oh how good it feels to take that negative energy from inside us and push it onto someone else.

It's exceptionally rare that these "feel-good" actions produce positive results toward our end goals in our corporate world. Worse, they can blind us to the potential consequences of those same actions. When someone gets so frustrated with a team or a manager that they spend three or four hours obsessing over whatever the incident was, they can't make impact on what's expected of them now—and that's something that will come up on their next performance appraisal. In addition to that, that *Goddamn angry email* they felt so justified sending after stewing on it for so long will likewise come back to haunt them.

Justification is seldom a good reason to do anything. It

usually only feeds our ego and seldom do we get a sense of satisfaction from actions taken to justify the why of an idea, opinion, or other action. We see this clearly in our next anti-pattern in adopting a pack-mule mentality.

PACK-MULE MENTALITY

Pack-mule mentality frequently kicks in when someone is coming up for promotion. They feel as if they are the only one who can get tasks done. They can't ask for help and they have something to prove. Meanwhile, true impact comes from leveraging the resources around you, whether it's people, time, funding, or flying monkeys. When we think we have to do it all ourselves, we are really putting blinders up that prevent us from seeing opportunities to scale our efforts to actually get to the next level of impact.

Granted, sometimes you have to be a pack mule because you're constrained by particular events. You may not be able to find someone to help on a project because you don't have the money to pay them. But when you find yourself thinking in that way, always take a deeper dive into the belief you're clinging to. Is it possible it's a false premise? Is it possible that you could try a different approach to find someone at a lower rate? A new avenue for capital? Are you sure there are no other options to help take the pressure off yourself?

In the extreme, pack-mule mentality creates the self-martyred victim. *I am suffering. I am making myself suffer and I want validation for that.* Suffering is the antithesis of making impact. When the Silicon Valley start-up hype was at its peak, there was this underlying theme that those people ignored their lives outside of work. They barely acknowledged their significant others. They didn't see their kids for three years. They created a successful start-up as they suffered personally. And now many of those people are looking back from the vantage point of second marriages and question why it was worth it. They see now that that's not how you're supposed to live life.

The pack-mule mentality is all about mis-prioritizing the motivations behind your efforts. Similar to that is the inability to prioritize your actions in general, which is our next anti-pattern to discuss.

The Inability to Prioritize

The inability to prioritize is related to multitasking. When we multitask and switch between tasks at a high frequency, it's often because we don't have the concept of prioritization down.

I'll sell my invention so that everyone can be superheroes. Everyone can be super! And when everyone's super...no one will be!
—SYNDROME (BUDDY PINE/INCREDIBOY)

Syndrome's idea in the Disney Pixar movie *The Incredibles* understands too well what equal prioritization means. While your goals may not be to turn everyone into superheroes to level out a hierarchy of specialness among beings, by not being able to prioritize your tasks you are leveling out the specialness of your goals.

If everything feels urgent and important, then we have an ever-increasing to-do list where every task listed needs equal time and energy and we get overwhelmed. We get stressed. Stress inhibits our ability to think clearly, to take the right actions, in short, it prevents us from making impact. (More about that in the next chapter.)

Being able to prioritize requires developing and knowing what our true goals are. They will be what we build our life around and prioritize our tasks around. In a hospital ER, they use the term triage to determine which patients will be seen first, which last, and which somewhere in between. There, urgent means there are going to be negative ramifications if a problem isn't solved ASAP. Important means there will be a negative side effect if this is not resolved in a larger timeframe, perhaps a day or a week. Everything after that is really just an inconvenience to have at the moment, "take two pain killers and call us in the morning."

If you can apply those terms to your own tasks, you'll get your urgent and important work done, then you can focus on the rest with a clearer mind. But in order to make use of a triage system where you tackle the urgent and important tasks first, you have to be willing and able to say no to other requests. If you've ever had trouble trying to figure out what prioritization looks like, this quote from Jack Handy sums it up perfectly:

To me, it's a good idea to always carry two sacks of something when you walk around. That way, if anybody says, "Hey, can you give me a hand?" you can say, "Sorry, got these sacks."

—*DEEPER THOUGHTS: ALL NEW, ALL CRISPY* (HACHETTE BOOKS 1993)

Our inability to prioritize ends our discussion on the common anti-patterns related to our behaviors that produce unimpactful actions. Next up is the final bucket: problems with our foundations.

PROBLEMS WITH OUR FOUNDATIONS

By foundations here, we're talking about our basic human skills:

· Our ability to control our emotions
· Our self-image
· Our biases
· Our grittiness

We all make decisions and take actions based on our unique positioning with those skills. Some of them we've sharpened, others we've left dull. When we overlook how critical it is to develop those core skills we do so at the detriment of our own personal and professional growth.

We are going to list some of the most common problems below but think of it this way: If the first time you ever negotiated for the funding of a project with a new VP that you don't know is also the first time you've ever negotiated for funding without a strong foundation, you'll be walking into a potential disaster. Your insecurity may cause you to misread her signs. You may lose your temper as you overcompensate to prove you know what you're doing. You may feel so discouraged in the middle of the meeting that you just give up.

When your foundational skills are weak, all actions built from them will be flawed, and that's what we're talking about here: about how your basic emotional skills drive your actions. If you delay mastering these skills, you do so at your own peril.

EMOTIONAL CONTROL

Our emotions help us make sense and understand the world around us. They give us love and art, they fuel amazing advances in technology, and they muck up everything we're doing right. Left unchecked, they make you do unimpactful actions and can create negative consequences: flying off the handle at a coworker over a small mistake, for example, or venting your frustration at your partner due to a small lapse in attention they had is another.

Both of those are relatively minor and can be smoothed down later, but what about when your emotions get so roiled up, road rage develops. You get distracted and slam into the car next to you. The accident not only makes you late for work where you miss an important meeting but now you're shelling out cash to cover insurance deductibles. So, while emotions are important, we have to understand blips in our control over them can cause large negative ramifications for our big-picture goals. A wrong word can destroy a relationship that took years to create. A lack of discretion in a comment to a VP can remove your potential for advancement. If you think about it, anger and envy can actually make you go bankrupt.

The good news is emotional havoc isn't inevitable. One of the goals of this book is to help you understand the source of your emotional responses, get them in check, and then use them for productive purposes instead. Gaining control of your emotions will help you feel more confident and develop a stronger self-image, which is also required for impactful actions.

SELF-IMAGE

Our self-image can create barriers that limit or even prevent us from taking action that makes impact. due to that self-image. If you have a negative view of yourself, for example, you might think you're a failure, so you adopt an I-can't-do-that mentality, which prevents you from even trying. Related to that is the self-image of a victim. We see that in people who grew up in a household with hypercritical parents. They become adults who find it hard to fathom that they're ever good enough to succeed. They believe they don't deserve success and their belief inhibits them from even trying.

Our self-image not only controls the size of the sandbox on the playground but it determines our place within it. There are people who have a goal to be the sandbox king—or maybe just a CTO—but have convinced themselves that it is completely outside their realm of thinking. That may be because they just don't find the position attractive. It might be because they aren't prone to that work style. Or it might be because they can't take themselves seriously enough to be in that kind of position. And that third one is due to a negative self-image that we want to get adjusted.

Meanwhile, we're perpetually bombarded with advice to "develop a growth mindset" or to take bold actions. Both are required to make positive impact but both require a healthy self-image. Everyone has the ability to adapt to their situation and take actions toward their goals by calming their negative needs and instead focusing on the task at hand. You must clear the emotional biases that weaken your foundation, and to do so, you must be aware of them.

WE'RE NOT AWARE OF OUR BIASES

Do you have biases against certain actions, ideas, places, or people? Are you aware of those biases as you're making decisions? Those are key questions to ask.

We're not discussing obvious biases here. Hopefully, you're above manifesting behavior based on biases against gender, skin color, sexual preference, or other discriminatory beliefs. Instead, we're talking about how you work with the other parts of your company. Do you groan in negative anticipation because you believe "those bean counters in accounting" won't approve funding? If so, you're demonizing a whole different work group and that makes it harder to work with them in each successive encounter you have.

When a designer approaches a programmer and says, "Hey! We need a giant explosion out of which comes a pink dinosaur dancing the macarena, okay?" and walks away because he doesn't want to hear the restrictions, he just knows the "stodgy" programmer is going to give him and he's setting himself up for a real-life explosion later. That's because the programmer, who already thinks none of the artists have a clue how difficult her job is, has resentment building.

"Ugh! The amount of freaking code I got to put in to make that thing happen, is almost impossible!" they complain. But they do so to themself and their team who agrees: the artists are clueless.

Meanwhile, thinking everything is possible and easy, the artists go completely off the rails in their design to the point that the macarena bit is now 80 percent of the performance budget on the screen, which means the whole team is criticized for being inefficient.

However, if the biases had all been checked at the door, things could have gone down differently. Going the extra step to see what it takes for the other to do their job is one way to conquer your bias. Understanding the pressures and expectations that are on them is another. And in doing so, everyone will be able to negotiate with each other and, hence, everyone gets to make impact.

If the programmer would have tugged on the artist's sleeve and asked, "Uh, like, uh, I know you want a dinosaur dancing and stuff, but like we kind of only have 5 percent of the budget now, and I need to ask you why you want that."

At which point the artist can explain that they just want

a huge cinematic element, which leaves the programmer options to find a more economical way of creating one. Budget is kept, the element is in, the entire project hits the goal, and everyone is happy because they made impact.

As you'll find over the course of this book, by assuming that those "bean counters" are allies, you'll learn how to play the game the right way and actually get the funding you want. You'll understand what they need in order to justify giving you the money. We have to be very aware of how we think about everyone we meet and every process we experience. We can't let our biases get in the way of keeping our foundation bucket filled with positive behaviors.

While we just discussed biases against others, there's another, equally important bias. It's a bias against effort or grit.

BEING GRITLESS

Grit, as modern psychological science identifies it, is the ability to push through difficult times. It's a matter of doing what needs to be done. Grit was an essential ingredient for the survival of your ancestors. To get an idea, just ask your grandparents how hard things were when they were growing up. Grit is about struggling against the odds, surviving in the face of adversity, and staying focused on a life goal, despite the world being on fire. Yes, that's the dramatic nature of your ancestors' grit. That's what they went through in order to make sure you're here today, reading this book.

In modern times, it's easy to be gritless. Our lifestyles take a lot for granted and can produce a system where, early on, you don't get a chance to develop strong patterns for having grit. And lacking skill development in the area of grit is a common problem when it comes to making impact.

As you define goals and work toward them, you will face a plethora of obstacles. Your skill level in grit will be the thing that pushes you through...or it won't. A low grit level means you'll be prone to giving up, not learning, or blaming failures on other situations.

A lack of grit can easily manifest itself into the sour-grapes mentality. That's when someone throws up their hands and declares, "Oh, that's too difficult! I never wanted to do it anyway." You see that in a lot of younger workers just starting out in their careers who realize they have to unclog the toilet in between the more glamorous aspects of their job.

Grit is one of the critical factors in achieving goals, but you can have it without actually having to be gritty. The secret in the sauce is finding that true goal that makes you wake up every morning saying, "Hey, I'm willing to shovel cow manure today because I know that clearing off this land is going to let me build my house on it later," or something else of that nature.

CHANGING COURSE

Grit winds up our discussion on problems with our foundation. It also winds up our discussion on the anti-patterns behind our unimpactful actions. And now that you know what the anti-patterns of behavior are behind your unimpactful actions, it's time to talk about why they are there and why you developed those anti-patterns.

It may seem surprising to learn that the root of those behaviors is actually found in the chemical reactions that happen inside our bodies in response to what happens around us. It's simple to say that our modern work lives are complex and stressful. We worry about deliverables, performance appraisals, or how someone in accounting seems to keep eating our lunch in the fridge.

Humans are social animals and, as such, we've developed finely designed systems to help us deal with survival in our social environments. Sadly, our modern environments don't match the patterns of our early humans but our biology hasn't caught up. Where those two worlds collide is a massive source of action-based-failure. It is, by far, the most common problem that I've seen in terms of keeping people from making an impact. It's so important, in fact, that we're going to spend the whole next chapter talking about it.

CHAPTER 3

IT'S NOT YOU, IT'S YOUR STRESS

As threatened in Chapter 1, we're going to take a look at the way chemicals in our bodies influence our behaviors. We understand most readers would appreciate a straight-forward business book chock-full of anecdotes followed up with things like *4 steps to make impact,* but we feel that would be a disservice to you. While this book *will* provide you with a Playbook (in Part II) for making impact, there's a catch: that playbook won't work unless you're able to create it based on an understanding of what's really motivating you to take any action.

Our emotions fuel our anti-patterns. We could say they motivate us to take action—either unimpactful or impactful. If we did say that we'd be speaking the truth, but if we dig a little deeper, we'd discover our emotions are only made possible by the chemical releases our bodies produce in response to our experiences. That's such a surprising concept to so many that we're going to risk redundancy here and say it again:

Our emotions are only made possible by the chemical releases our bodies produce in response to our experiences.

Because our hormones and other neurological responses create our emotions and because our emotions are responsible for the anti-patterns that form our unimpactful actions, then that means (insert drumroll here) the number-one contributing factor to actions that hurt your goals is *not* tied to any external factors directly but instead is based on how your body, at chemical and neurological levels, responds to those factors and how you, at the brain level, take action on those reactions.

The good news is that you can learn to turn it all around, get control of your responses (or at least grow a little more aware of them), and learn to make impactful actions with the Playbook. To do that, we'll need to look at the hardware human beings have been running on for the past 200,000 years or so. In particular, we're going to focus on the stress response, which has been the backbone of our behaviors ever since we first stood up and heard the cracks from stretching our spines.

ACUTE STRESS

Robert M. Sapolsky's cornerstone book *Why Zebras Don't Get Ulcers* presents a basis for stress-related illness from the perspective of a biologist. It's a fantastic resource to help explain how stress gets in the way of making impactful actions. Please ask a real scientist or read his book if you want a more thorough description than you're about to find here.

As mentioned previously, the human body has been running on specialized hardware for the past couple of millennia. However, that hardware got its start a few million years before that when other organisms began developing the ability to exist and breed. In fact, the refinement of the nervous system, hormones, and stressors have been working to survive ever since the inception of life on Earth—yes, even amoebas had a stress response that helped them survive. Perhaps it's important to note here that your existence is proof of how good those systems have become.

Now, in the twenty-first century, your human body has a plethora of systems that release chemicals in order to function. Some systems release chemicals within your brain while others work in the bloodstream, and yet others in a system we have yet to name makes your heart go *BOOM-BOOM-BOOM* when a certain someone makes eye contact with you.

Basically, it's through releasing chemicals that your body *does stuff*. All day long and all night too, as you breathe, blink, or scratch your dog behind her ear, chemicals at work make your muscles move, your reflexes reflect, and your tummy rumble when you're hungry. As fantastic as all that sounds, what is most interesting is how your body releases chemicals when you experience stress.

Now, stress is a common thing. And from a scientific perspective, the word "stress" takes on specific meanings, which we're just going to gloss over here and call "stuff that makes you feel nervous, anxious, or uncomfortable." But not all stress is bad. Your body and mind expect and actually need a certain amount of stress to stay in balance. In fact, having the right levels of stress in a person's life has been shown to be the key for unlocking creative potential. However, when you become overly stressed, that is when you are experiencing what is referred to as *acute stress* and chemicals are released in your body in abundance.

Acute stress triggers a deluge of chemicals that helps your body with what is frequently called the flight, fight, or freeze response. That's when your system is primed to exert a lot of energy, really fast, for a short period of time. It does so with the expectation that you're about to need some life-saving energy. Let's say you're walking to your car in the mall parking lot when the pavement breaks open and out pops a demon with a mullet hairstyle and wearing an Elvis bedazzled jumpsuit. Your body will respond in a nanosecond. Your heart rate, blood pressure, and breathing rate will spike to transport nutrients and oxygen at greater rates while glucose is released into your muscles to provide enough energy to skedaddle.

It's really important to point out that once your body triggers this state of over-stress, it's not thinking long term. The acute-stress response is for emergency situations only. Your body is trying to optimize for survival at this point so it's releasing these hormones to get you out of immediate danger. When your body is going through this, it does not care about the past or the future. Its only concern is surviving the present moment and when that moment is over, then it's focused on surviving the next moment. Rinse and repeat.

That immediate response and myopic focus make a lot of sense when you're in imminent danger. It's smart to hold off on the long-term projects until you know there is a long term. If there's a tornado bearing down on the house, that's the time to head to the basement. It's not the time to break open cans of paint and start brushing Mandarin Tequila Sunrise orange all over the garage walls.

Now then, your body isn't just pumping out chemicals to get you to make a run from a demon with bad taste, it knows more resources are at play here. So during acute stress, chemicals turn down a bunch of systems because they are considered long-term projects, which helps save energy for the survival stuff. Digestion falls into that category. Your body figures there isn't enough time to derive the energetic benefits of the slow process of digestion, so why waste energy on it now? The same thing goes for growth and reproduction—both are energy expensive and relatively optimistic things to be worried about doing with your body.

While these chemicals are creating a focus that narrows down your physical state to only the bare basics, it has an effect on your mental state as well. In essence, chemicals give you tunnel vision. Because your entire body is focused on one thing—and the *entire body* includes your brain—when you're in acute stress, you're in no position to make long-term decisions. And that's when things start to go sideways in our modern world.

Remember, the acute-stress response of flight, fight, or freeze appeared eons ago to protect us from imminent danger. Probably not from demons nostalgic for the 1970s but from things like wild animals attacking us. Once we experienced the fearful stimuli, we'd hotfoot it across the plain, which would cause the extra chemicals to burn through our system and empty out. By the time we got back to the cave, we'd forget about the attack and be calmed down enough to draw pictures on the cave walls that would confuse future generations.

Our modern world is a bit different than the one in which these systems were developed. Our ancestors had to deal with mostly physical threats, while we mostly deal with mental and sociological ones. But here's the kicker: all that hardware is still running. Our stress systems will kick into high gear as though our stressors are physical issues. Consider how it feels when you get an angry email from your manager, a letter from the IRS, a report card for your kid that assures you he will never move out of your basement? Those events trigger the same flight, fight, or freeze response a saber-toothed tiger triggered in your ancestors once upon a time.

So we need to understand that with every blood pressure spike, we immediately stop caring about the future. We need to remember that our decision-making process shuts down every time we feel a surge of energy to tackle something when we watch the news.

Think about it: how many times a day do things set us off? Traffic, social media, work responsibilities, home responsibilities, all that nonstop stress is releasing loads of tunnel-vision-inducing chemicals in our bodies. More and more are pouring in but we don't have a savannah to run across to burn them out. And that means, we live our days in an almost chronic state of acute stress without ever releasing it. Our stress prevents us from thinking clearly. It induces fear, overwhelm, anger, and other emotions within us that then skew our perspectives and dictate the choices we make. When our mood and emotions are filters, the more negative they are, the more restrictive and less impactful they make us.

MOOD AND EMOTION ARE FILTERS

Humans, it can be argued, have the most advanced and complex chemical-emotion reactions to date, but it's been a work in progress for millennia. And today's reptiles very much represent how the first living organisms on our planet processed their world through chemicals and emotions. It's important to understand this because by understanding it, you can take better control of how you process your world. And taking control of it is how you make impactful actions.

We'll begin our lesson by talking about the green anole.

Stretched out on a smooth rock, a male anole bobs his head and appears to be staring off into space. The telltale red dewlap extending and contracting beneath his chin reveals he's on a mission. His reptilian brain has one goal in mind: attract a female. The air is dry, the wind is still, and the sun is warm. It's the perfect day for finding lizard love. But then a quick shadow passes over him. In a flash, our little anole is gone. He hides in a cluster of leaves while a kestrel falcon swoops overhead, shrieking *eeek eeek eeek* in disappointment. It was sure it had spied a tasty green meal from high above.

No longer remembering why he had gone to the rock to begin with, our lizard friend waits for his heart to return to a relaxed and steady beat, completely unaware he'd zipped past a small female anole munching on a fly as he sought shelter.

You might now recognize that what happened to the green anole lizard was a typical flight, fight, or freeze response. His brain sensed danger and released chemicals into his body. The chemicals screamed, "BE AFRAID" and fueled by adrenaline that set all systems at "go" for escape, he found refuge in an instant. Because his brain couldn't process *escape* along with anything else, all thoughts about finding a female or enjoying the sunshine were shut down. The point here is that survival has been hard-wired into the immediate reactions of our lizard example. Survival is so important, that its body is designed to sense danger and release chemicals, which better enable it to scurry away from that danger. Evolution has taught our lizard friend an important lesson: if you can't outrun the kestrel, mating season doesn't matter.

These same chemicals allow another reaction to occur, which is to "freeze." Most species who have to worry about getting eaten have adapted fantastic defensive strategies, including advanced camouflage. When danger appears, rather than running, they may choose to stay as still as possible, blending into the environment around them, making them hard to find or see. This pause is intentional. Much like the famous scene in *Jurassic Park*, a predator with poor eyesight has a weakness that its prey can exploit by simply staying still.

Moving up the food chain, we see a third behavior emerge: fight. The same chemicals that enabled our creatures to run from danger, or to stay perfectly still, can also be used to attack an aggressor or to bring down larger prey. Fight is an exceptionally advanced behavior and by far the riskiest. An animal is intentionally putting itself in danger in order to survive so it can mate or eat, two things that are so important, that it's worth the risk to get into the boxing ring that is really the bank of the river. Once again, the chemical release signals to the body to shut down any processing that's not involved with the fight at hand.

What we see in all three scenarios is more and more advanced behavior, given by the release of very similar chemicals. It's simplest to avoid the danger by moving away from it. That's easy and straightforward. More advanced is not to run but pause; keep an eye on the danger but don't play into its hands. This is showing higher-order processing and decision-making: there might be a risk in running right now so be patient. Finally, we see the most advanced of the three. Having to employ a risk-to-reward ratio to decide to engage in a conflict is higher-order decision-making. But we still haven't made it to humans, yet.

Moving up the evolution chain, we continue to see the same chemicals getting released but with much more complex behaviors involved. We see this in a gorilla thumping his chest to show a young gorilla who's boss. The older male saw the younger flirt with one of the favorite females and sensed his power and dominance in the group was threatened by the punk. In response, a surge of testosterone coursed through the older guy's veins, impulsively making him thump loudly on his chest, which translates loosely to: *Take me on! I dare you!* Perhaps that shoots a bit of fear through the youth and his adrenalin sends him scampering up a tree, out of the way. This is refined higher-order reasoning. Rather than engage in a fight, the older male chose to display his superiority to avoid a conflict.

Chemicals, pauses, and impulsive body language work well enough for most social animals, but we humans needed something better. We ramped it up several notches when our cognitive power introduced abstract thinking and the spoken word, but we didn't do it at the expense of all that came before.

Now, most neuroscientists are pretty much in agreement that our brains are composed of three parts. One harkens way back to the olden times and is a bit of a reptilian brain; it controls all automatic responses and regulates the body. Like the anole lizard, it is pretty much only instinctual. On top of that is part two, which is more like the gorilla brain. It's the mammalian or limbic brain and governs feeling and emotion. Atop that is part three, the neocortex (neo meaning new and cortex meaning bark or outer layer—remember the bark.) This top part is responsible for controlling cognition and for language.

Aside from the bark, it's also important to remember that the three parts of the brain are separate parts. While they communicate with one another, they evolved separately and don't work in conjunction with one another very well. The human brain needed to create ways for each layer to "interpret" the processes occurring on each of the other layers. This is why during the climactic scene of your favorite superhero movie, you suddenly feel moved to tears, or have abundant "go get 'em" energy after the movie is let out. Experiencing the joy and excitement of the characters in the movie is causing your body to respond as though it was the one in that stressful situation; your body dumped the same chemicals that would make you flight, fight, or freeze.

This concept is critical to how we're going to discuss your impact in this book, so we're going to take a second to drill into this a bit more. As humans, we're apex predators, meaning we really don't have to wake up and be afraid of some large thing eating us. But the hardware inside of us that used to be worried about that is still there. And it can't tell the difference between a *real* dinosaur chasing you down, or an angry email from your boss at work. In both cases, your body senses danger, and boom, chemical release.

However, as more complex creatures, we don't just sense those basic chemical dumps, w*e perceive them through a filter of what we call "emotion,"* which gives us a wonderful cascade of more states to exist in than our simple fish-based ancestors. You might hate and love something at the same time or be glad something is completed but sad that it's over. They're emotions that are more difficult to understand than flight, fight, or freeze and almost impossible to communicate to those around you.

Because you are human, and that means you are a social animal, you want to express how you're feeling, but that separation thing in the brain makes it difficult to do. Since they are two separately working parts, your limbic brain and your neocortex communicate in different code. Your limbic, where your emotions are raging, is on the opposite side of the somewhat soundproof bark in your brain from your neocortex, where language and thinking happen. So translating your emotions into words is tricky.

Ramping it up a notch, if you think expressing your own

emotions is hard, compound that by trying to understand the emotional communication of other people. This is such a common enigma that there's a whole industry of rom-com movies based entirely around the concept of misunderstanding the complex emotions of another person.

The neocortex must guess what the feelings mean by thinking up rational reasons for them. And that's why you rant about how crappy the ending of the Netflix show is, about how disappointed you are in the writing of it, when really, you're angry at yourself for wasting six hours on the couch when you could have been doing something productive and fun.

That third part of our brain has served humans well. We've used it to create an amazing world filled with wondrous art, technology, and everything in between. However, because our thinking is separate from our emotions, there is a perpetual internal friction that the rest of the animals do not have. The lizard, deer, gorilla, and all the others will feel their fear, joy, or anger for a brief time and then let them go to resume whatever they were doing before the inciting incident aroused that emotional response. But we humans often don't give ourselves that luxury.

When we feel an emotion, it doesn't disappear as it does in our other animal friends. The chemicals continue to pulse through our bodies because we dwell on whatever happened. We play it over in our heads again and again. Inevitably, the fear or anger we were feeling gets intensified as we continue to ruminate. So we vent and we rant some more. We post on social media where other people who feel the same way add in their own emotional responses and then we symbiotically reinforce one another's anger.

All that communicating, because we are so focused on what we think we feel, winds up being a perpetual inciting incident that only encourages the emotional response even more. We just don't let our emotions go with ease—even when what we're thinking and ranting about has nothing to do with what we were really feeling. Sometimes we carry on so much, that long past a moment of danger, we remain in a constant state of anxiety. Or we become so embroiled in our anger, we destroy one relationship after another and miss goal after goal.

So you see how our chemical reactions influence our ability to take impactful actions toward reaching our goals.

AN EXERCISE IN ANGER

There are numerous studies and clinical research regarding how emotions can hurt our ability to evaluate what's impactful and achieve it. As it turns out, the emotion of anger literally warps our worldview.

In 2013 the *National Forum Journal of Counseling and Addiction* released research on how anger affects the human body. You just learned about how hormones and neurotransmitters are released when you're stressed, the same kind of thing happens when you're angry. But with anger, there is a twist.

When we get angry, that influx of chemicals not only creates a tunnel vision effect, but it does a few other things too. One, it makes it difficult to understand anyone other than yourself. Two, something akin to a self-preservation reflex kicks in and makes it impossible to think we could be wrong. And three, even worse, it makes us want to get close to whatever is angering us so we can kill it.

Yes, kill it.

Historically, it makes sense that we would be programmed to destroy whatever is angering us. You could even say it is a fundamental, important part of our survival. When something attacks you, anger is generated so that you don't feel bad taking its life to save your own. Anger is what allowed us to defend the people we love against attackers scaling the castle walls. If our bodies didn't shut down our ability to reason when we get angry while the armed warriors were leaping over the ramparts to sack our village, we might stand by idly and let them destroy everything, having analyzed the situation, and decided that perhaps they were very hungry. Besides, didn't we do the same to them the previous winter?

The thing is, we don't need marauding rivals threatening to destroy our surplus wheat to set us off into a tailspin of anger. It can be something as simple as getting an email from Todd that pisses you off because you think he's dissing you.

You read the email, decide he's an arrogant fool, and tear off down the hallway to tell him so. Anger is preventing you from double-checking to see if he really was disrespectful in the email. It has you convinced you are right and he is, without question, an idiot. You have no ability to process differing logic or to evaluate if the path you're taking to correct the perceived injustice is correct.

At its core, this state can cause us to take actions that feel correct in the moment because they are driven by a false sense of perspective. But they're not the right actions. They are unimpactful ones. Ergo, anger is the enemy of impact.

So when you get an email and you feel angry, even though your body is convincing you that attacking the sender is the best thing you can do right now, period, it's not. Here's where the concept of "let cooler heads prevail" is legitimate. If you give your body a chance to process the anger chemicals and release them, then you start to strategize and think clearly.

GET SOME CONTEXT: STORYTIME WITH COLT

Robert got a lesson in how unimpactful anger could be early on in his career. He was brilliant at his job and was up for a principal engineering role at a video game company. In his world, principal engineering positions are the apex; you can't go higher than that in his division. He was only twenty-five at the time, which was an age for a principal engineer that was unheard of.

He went through the process of doing all the work and whatever was necessary to achieve the role, and he was confident he'd get it. He had an "in" in HR who had promised him it was in the bag and was only a matter of time before the announcement was made. A few of the perks that came with the position started coming to him too. He knew he was a shoo-in for the position.

But then he got hit with a bad, lingering, head cold while dealing with some stressful stuff going on in his family. Work became his escape from the mess he didn't want to deal with at home but, really, he shouldn't have been there. His energy was low. His emotions were all over the place.

One morning when he was particularly in a down place, he received an email where someone told him there was a problem with the code he wrote. He immediately reacted with a defensive reply. "Bullshit! That's not how that code works. You don't know what you're talking about." Soon afterward, the reply came in—a calm reply—that says the person did some research and, yes, there was a problem with the code. He explained what was going on and said, "This is a problem that people are experiencing, and I need you to fix it."

Robert felt his head explode. He stormed over to the person's desk and proceeded to egg him into a screaming argument. Because they were in an open-desk area, everybody in the area heard it. Possibly everybody within a three-mile radius outside the building too.

Three weeks later, Robert received an email from the owner of the company that let him know he was being passed over for the principal engineering position. The owner had heard about the yell-fest through the grapevine and said he didn't think principal engineers should conduct themselves that way.

Had Robert been in a different place when he'd read the email, the whole situation might not have happened. But by not managing his emotions, by not understanding that being in that state made him defensive and angry, he didn't question whether it was right to explode on someone trying to fix a problem.

Oh, and by the way, there really was a problem with the code.

Thankfully, Robert learned from his mistakes, which is the important thing. We all have and will continue to screw things up. But if you learn from them, then that's okay. If you don't, then that kind of makes you bad at being human. Unfortunately, anger and stress can become so perpetual that you don't give yourself the opportunity to learn anything from it. And becoming addicted to those emotions will only lead you further and further away from being able to make impact.

ADDICTED TO STRESS

We all know somebody who can't get off social media. They're angry every day. When you ask them what's going on in their life, they either rant about some injustice or another or they say things like, "Oh my God! I couldn't get out of bed today. I was just too exhausted to face the world." Meanwhile, you know the person slept in until noon and you're wondering what on earth could be wrong with them.

Given what we discovered in the previous chapter, an anger addiction might have something to do with it.

At the risk of angering any biologists who are reading this book, we're going to take some time to discuss a couple of chemicals released during acute-stress situations: the stress hormones adrenaline and cortisol. When we're faced with a threat or stressor, adrenaline is what our body immediately releases to get the surge of energy to fly, fight, or freeze going. Cortisol is released a little after that to help maintain resources while the stress occurs. It's cortisol that slows down your digestive system and releases sugar into your bloodstream for energy.

Cortisol is necessary for our survival and good health. It even does things like help us wake up in the morning. Adrenaline is what gives us the boost of energy we need to jump away from an oncoming, out-of-control Vespa. However, as wine, dark chocolate, and movie theater popcorn proves over and over: too much of a good thing is a very bad thing. In the case of stress hormones, when they are perpetually released into our system because of chronic stress, the good it does they do is far outweighed by the bad.

Now it's important to note that your body is really great at adapting to things. When you combine that concept with the law of diminishing return, which denotes how the human brain takes less pleasure over time from something it repeatedly receives, you find the crux where the hormones wreak havoc in our bodies. As with any other chemical dependence, once your body adapts to high levels of them, over time, you will be driven to seek larger and larger doses to get the results you desire.

Before you start thinking that the previous paragraph has nothing to do with stress, please be assured it does. You see, most people don't realize how stressed they are. When they are flying into a constant state of outrage every day, their body gets used to a certain level of hormones. The body also starts to adapt the rest of the systems to make that high level your new baseline. So over time, repeated exposure to stressful situations can cause your body to crave the stress hormones in order to keep its adapted equilibrium.

Yes, we're saying that, effectively, there's a biological precedent for the behavior we see in people who are continuously upset at everything around them. (But that doesn't mean we should condone their behavior.) We all know someone who seems to be outraged every day at a new problem. Or they can't seem to let go of a long-ago transgression regardless of how minor it is in their life now. Hard as we try, we can't seem to get them to unstick themselves from their outrage.

Currently, we're seeing the first generation to grow up on social media struggle because their skin isn't thick enough to handle the world around them. They feel that everything is a crisis of existence. Granted, there does seem to be a higher-than-normal level of injustice and sadness in the world, thus some validity to their response. But you can see very clear behavioral patterns among them: there is a constant outrage cycle that keeps them from being able to see out of the chaos. They lack the ability to make impact, their physical health suffers and yet the first thing they do each morning is log onto the social network. Observers of this behavior could easily draw a conclusion that many are addicted to getting upset.

This trend is one of the reasons that the modern internet (social media, specifically) is so dangerous to developing minds. The engagement system that has been built for those platforms recognizes that things like outrage and fear cause this chemical release and dependency. So algorithms keep them tuned in and angry. In essence, we have a new form of adrenaline junkies who wanna feel the rush. But here, it's getting hooked on outrage.

Now then, remember, during acute stress, your body releases these hormones because it wants—and expects—you to use them to run away from the attacking tiger or to fight off the troll who sprang up from under the bridge. But if you're sitting at your computer, raging at the internet and not following it up by a 400-meter sprint, then those chemicals are sitting in your system with nothing to do but slowly tear down your tissues. On the plus side, at least you're not a salmon.

Salmon are born literally under a rock in some freshwater river. When they're about a year old, they get adventurous and head downstream to frolic in the wide, blue ocean. At some point, they get a little homesick and decide to return to their old stomping grounds where hopefully they can meet up with some old friends and breed. The trip back requires a strenuous and stressful trip, fighting the current to go upstream. Most salmon only go home once. That's because it's such a stressful adventure that the salmon die at the end of it due to an over-release of cortisol. The stress hormone degrades their systems to the point where nothing functions appropriately. At the end of their journey, their tissues break down, and the circle of life continues.

We non-salmon humans thankfully have resources to deal with the stress. Deep breathing, meditation, exercise all will help. Secondly, we have to recognize how stress influences our mental state and then take responsibility for our stress load. Sure, there is a whole set of stressors thrust upon us: sick children, looming deadlines, the Superbowl, etc. But engaging in gossip, social media, watercooler chat, or binge-watching trashy reality TV are stressors we choose to involve ourselves in—or not. Each of these can trigger our stress hormones to release. Their existence is nonnegotiable but how much we engage and how we react to it is something we must take control over.

PART II

LEARN WHAT
IT TAKES

CHAPTER 4

ESTABLISH A SOLID FOUNDATION

The Australian tiger beetle is the fastest bug on the planet. Less than an inch long, it can travel over eight feet in a second, which may not sound like much, but if you apply its size-to-speed ratio to humans, which would be the equivalent of over 435 miles per hour. In fact, its speed is so fast for its size that its brain can't comprehend and take in all the sights and sounds around it when it moves. There's this mismatch in its ability to move versus its ability to sense what's in its environment while moving.

In order to keep from smashing into walls and rocks, or zooming into the mouth of a predator, it zips at near-teleporting speed for a blip of time then stops dead to figure out where it is. When the brain catches up, it zips to the next stop. And that's how it lives its life: zip, stop, and reorient; zip, stop, and reorient.

The behavior of the tiger beetle is a cautionary tale on our path to creating impact. Many of us are so focused on the work, executing at full velocity, that we don't stop to evaluate our new position and re-orient ourselves. The result? Smacking up against something we could have easily seen, causing all sorts of delays and a bit of bruised ego. Much like the tiger beetle, we need to be able to periodically stop in the middle of our haste in order to refine our direction to ensure we're still going along the right path. We'd be able to attack our tasks with energy and force and then stop and evaluate, which would give us a rest, so we can retackle and get back at it.

In Chapter 2, you learned how problems in your foundation bucket create roadblocks to reaching your goals. Establishing a solid foundation by getting control of your emotions allows you to have the ability to move from thought through to action—action that makes impact, action based on reason and research, action that moves you toward your goal. Acknowledging you *can* do that is the first step to becoming a student of impact. The second step then is *learning how* to do that.

The how part comes in the form of harnessing the energy that negative experiences give us and using it for good.

Once we realize and fully understand the stress-response and anger-response system inside us, then we can take actions to counteract it. Like the tiger beetle, when we feel triggered we can stop, re-evaluate, and then use logic to decide if we really need to jump into the fray or pursue more appealing goals.

Once we realize that emotions are the source of these negative urges, we can choose to rationalize and change our attitude before we respond by commandeering our emotions, learning to get mental space, surveying our emotions, and embracing our strengths to find a blissful balance.

RATIONALIZE AND CHANGE YOUR ATTITUDE

Now that we've taken a small look into how the body works with respect to chemicals and how that can define your mood, we need to talk about where perception fits in. Because sure, "chemicals happen," but when you stop there, simply admitting they produce emotional responses, it's easy to give up. You'll adopt the motto *I'm a slave to my emotions*. The thing is you don't have to be. You can change your motto to *I'm a master of my emotions*. And you do that by adapting a different perspective.

Perception—use it or lose it.

—RICHARD BACH

Inherent in the definition of perception is the concept that what we perceive is our personal version of reality, that it is of our own creation. Because it is yours, you get to take responsibility for it, which means you can control it for your own benefit. And you do that by manipulating your emotions.

As we just learned, our unhelpful emotions can lead to unimpactful actions. Meanwhile, it's our logic that fuels our impactful ones—thinking things through, researching, learning from others in lieu of learning by experience. When we want to stop the anti-patterns behind our unimpactful behavior, a good place to start is with our emotions.

But perhaps we've been too obtuse; let's give a concrete example. Eating cake for dinner. Logically, you know serving yourself a seven-layer chocolate cake every night is not a healthy thing. There are too many calories, too much sugar, and the eggs whipped into it don't supply enough protein. Yet you still indulge. Perhaps you're relishing the decadence. Perhaps you're loving how you're thumbing your nose at rules and expectations by eating it so frequently. Perhaps you're not sure why, you just do it because it feels good. So you eat it. Every night. But you don't want to. You're not happy with how tight the waistbands of all your trousers are becoming. You want to stop and start eating salads but you just can't seem to find the willpower.

Simple wanting isn't enough to make you change habits—

unless the emotion is strong enough behind the wanting. And logic certainly isn't enough. You've known all along daily massive doses of chocolate cake are bad for you. So you need to change your perspective at the emotional level to make it undesirable. One way to do that is with storytelling.

You could spend some time every day visualizing a story of something disgusting related to eating cake. Perhaps someone perpetually sneezes over each cut piece. Perhaps someone with Montezuma's revenge just...well, never mind, you get the picture. Just imagine the scene so intently that you insert yourself into a palpable feeling of disgust throughout your body. Do that frequently enough and you'll realize your desire for cake for dinner has evaporated. By triggering the emotional brain, you tapped into your lower self, thus creating what you wanted: pants that fit again.

LESSONS FROM HELL'S TRAINER

In 2012, *Men's Health* magazine featured an article written by Andrew Heffernan, CSCS, and Stacy Kranitz about a mysterious trainer whom world-class athletes sought out for his mystical powers. He's referred to as Hell's Trainer, though his given name is Frank Matrisciano.

Matrisciano has perfected the art of manipulating your emotions to spur your body to conquer what seem impossible feats. Ever wonder why NBA stars continue to drive to the basket despite being in a state of utter exhaustion? It's very possible they've been under the Hell's Trainer's tutelage. He's worked with numerous NBA players.

What Matrisciano does is imbue his training sessions with visualizing techniques. The visualizing here, though, is not of the warm and fuzzy kind. He doesn't encourage you to picture yourself hoisting a loving-cup trophy and basking in the adulation of a giant crowd. Quite the opposite. After you've done endless laps on a track, or rounds upon rounds of push-ups, when you're at the point where your body is screaming for relief and about to collapse from sheer exhaustion, he yells in your face. He insists something horrible is happening that hits you in the heart. Maybe it's about your newborn son being trapped in a house on fire. Or it's about your mom—she's fallen and is unconscious on a subway rail with a train barreling down on her.

Whoever is closest to you, whatever is sacred to you, he'll use it to implant a terrifying situation in your brain. You picture it, and even though your body was previously telling you it was at the point of no return, suddenly it's spurred on with energy to go another round. Remember the chemical surge that happens with stress—that's what Matrisciano creates with those images.

When athletes get trained like that, their perception of what their bodies can do changes. They realize they can do so much more, push harder, run faster, whatever their sport requires of them at a higher level of performance than they had thought possible before. So later, when there are just seconds left in the last quarter and they are dribbling down the court feeling as if they can't make it to the other side, they can tap into the memory that says, *hey, I'm unlimited* and make the layup.

The particular technique Hell's Trainer uses might seem a bit on the overkill side for some who are not professional athletes. But what he's doing is basically the same process as visualizing negative situations for the chocolate cake. It's harnessing the power of emotions to change your behavior by changing your beliefs or attitude about a particular situation. That's just one way to manipulate your emotions to make impact.

Another way is on the quieter side.

ZEN AND THE ART OF DECISION-MAKING

As we've just shown, Hell's Trainer is great for changing your perspective so you can change your behaviors from unimpactful to impactful. But it may be a difficult approach for changing the way you handle emails from the infamous Todd (remember him...the coworker who infuriates you with every email?). Instead, you might want to go a little Zen with that one.

Buddhists work for years to clear their minds. Yet somehow, they can be the most insightful decision-makers possible. That's because by keeping the mind clear, they stay away from the baser instincts, leaving room for the higher-order and rational thoughts.

Granted, it's easier to achieve that clear mind when you're in a monastery or living as a hermit atop a beautiful mountain than it is when you're spending your days staring at a computer monitor, feeling the pressures of job, family, school, and whatever it was you had for lunch that didn't agree with you. But we're not saying you need to abandon it all and hop on a plane to Tibet. We are saying that if we can emulate the Zen way of finding mental space just a little, we'll be less apt to fly off the handle.

We'll get into more details later in the Playbook when we discuss the need to buy time. For now, we want you to think about making dinner. No, not the chocolate-cake dinner. A real one with healthy portions of protein sources, vegetables, and that sort of thing. Imagine getting home from work a little frazzled from traffic and you're rushing to get dinner made because your book club is meeting later.

In your hurry and rush, you spill tomato sauce or you drop an egg on the floor. At that point, you have two options for perspective. One: you can say screw it and order a pizza, have a beer, and sulk for the rest of the night, which makes book club almost unbearable. Two: you can get some mind space for rational thought by taking a minute to breathe and allow the anger chemicals to dissipate. Then you'll be able to remind yourself that dinner is only part of the evening. You can tap into the fun you expect to have at book club, which will make cleaning up easier now and a more enjoyable evening later.

In other words, you need to learn the art of letting cooler heads prevail. If you give your body the chance to disperse the chemicals that produce the anger or stress, the negative emotion that comes with them will dissolve as well. Then you'll be able to tap into reason, remember the ultimate goal, gain the perspective that Todd's email is just a blip in your day, and move on.

We humans are heliocentric creatures. Navel-gazing is a natural tendency for us, which is great if we're doing it in a way that makes us better or helps us find more joy. But when we spend too much time thinking about our own injuries, scars, and how we've been wronged, nothing good comes from that. We can't make impact on any of our goals when we stay mired in righteous anger. Crap is always going to happen. Until we can learn to rise above it, to take the time to see the bigger picture, our attempts to make progress will be thwarted.

Now let's talk about some actions you CAN take to help with this.

ATTITUDE CHECK

Changing your perception so that you can rationalize negative events before you take action is the first step toward becoming a Student of Impact. The next is being aware of how your attitude is slanting your perceptions of events and other people.

Again, we're asking you to do something that is easier said (written and read) than done. What makes giving yourself an attitude check even harder is that your day-to-day life keeps you too close to things and people to really be able to tell if your perception of them is skewed. You can't quickly and easily find an Archimedean Point where you can perceive what's happening to you and around you with a view of totality. But there are always opportunities to catch glimpses of your attitude in action.

You can see it in how you judge people once they are out of your presence. Are you quick to focus on their negative qualities and bad opinions? Or are you more generous and forgiving when it comes to their flaws?

You will see definite signs of your attitude in how you face adversity or resistance. Are you quick to forget or gloss over any mistakes on your part? Do you instinctively blame others for any negative things that happen to you?

Happy people don't change. If you're happy with something, you're incentivized to maintain it and make no changes. So if you've answered any of the above questions with negativity-tinged responses, then perhaps your attitude could use some fine-tuning to help you get into a more positive, solution-oriented frame of mind for making impact, which is very possible if you believe in the supreme power of your attitude to alter your circumstances.

See, you are not a pawn in a game controlled by others. You are an active player who can move the pieces at will and even rewrite the rules. Letting your emotions control you and having a negative worldview are the primary things that keep you from making impact. As we saw in the previous section, you can control your emotions, and here, we're presenting ways to improve your attitude.

FIND YOUR JOY BENEATH THE SURFACE

As we all endeavor to work toward our goals, it's critical that we understand the deeper reason why a particular form of work calls to us or creates happiness for us. On the surface, many of us will claim our goals are self-evident: *I do X because X is obviously awesome*. But this can create problems as the world around you changes. What if you aren't allowed to do X anymore or what if you have to move to a new role that requires you to do Y instead? You should expect this to happen a number of times on the path to your goals, so it's important that you don't get discouraged or feel downtrodden when it happens.

The trick to surviving these types of changes is to dig deeper than the surface and ask some tough questions: What about your actions, job, skills, or goals really makes you love doing it? Can you distill it down to an action, or set of actions, instead of roles or responsibilities?

For example, explorers have always been touted as a source of discovery and inspiration. From the outside, it's easy to idolize their work. How amazing would it be to discover new lands and see new things for the first time? Sadly though, we often find that's not usually their underlying motivation. The large majority of explorers were in it for the cold, hard cash, and a few of the greats were just not inclined to want to be around other humans.

When you combine those true motivations, you realize that the base goal of "make money and don't be annoyed by humans" could allow these persons to switch careers at any time, as long as those core goals were being met.

As such, it's very important to reframe your perspective so that you're looking for the joy in what's beneath the surface—you must "find the joy in the process," as I've been known to say. Once you can harness the realization that where your joy lies is the place where you can pivot to any new job, role, or need, as long as you can find your core joy. The stronger your sense of identity in this space, the more resilient you'll be to change, and the easier it'll be to achieve your goal.

RECOGNIZE EMOTIONAL TRIGGERS

At the risk of making your head explode over more talk about your emotions, we want to insert something here about how managing emotional triggers can help change your attitude for the better.

Negative emotions thrive on ignorance. The moment you are aware of how they operate and dominate you is the moment they lose their hold on you and can be tamed. It's important to survey and understand your triggers in order to keep yourself in a state of rationality. This is where your Zen moments will come in handy; finding some mental space is how you can begin to respond in a rational way. It will allow you to take a peek inside to catch that emotional self in action and reflect on how you operate under stress.

When triggered, try to see if you can determine what particular weaknesses come out in such a moment. Learn to ask yourself questions like: Why am I feeling anger or resentment here? Where does this need for attention come from? Is it the desire to please, to bully, or to control? Is it a deep level of mistrust?

Under such scrutiny, you can look at the decisions you make when triggered—especially those that have been ineffective. When you do, can you see a pattern of an underlying insecurity that impels them or is there something else?

Let's try to put this in action and pretend you recently solved a long-standing, irritating problem. You kind of did it by accident—it's more like you stumbled upon a solution than actually figured it out. But whatever. It's done! We can all stop complaining now. But then, as you're walking out the building at the end of the day, Kyle, who you think has a big head because he's on a team renown for solving the *big* problems nods goodbye and says, "Good job. I didn't know you could do something like that." How does that make you feel?

Do you want to grab him by the shirt collar and demand he explains himself? *What do you mean? Of course I can do that kind of work!* If so, why do you feel the anger? If you survey yourself, does the anger come from fear over thinking maybe you're inadequate at your job, that if you hadn't accidentally fixed it, you never would have? If that's the case, your anger is based on insecurity. And if *that's* so, then very possibly your insecurity has your attitude a bit skewed to being defensive around people like Kyle who get all the difficult problems because they are *that* good. Maybe your attitude is the one making you think he has a big head.

On the other hand, does his response make you swell

with pride because one of the top guns noticed you had potential? If so, that will encourage you to approach him with gratitude for his comment and an entrée to a potential mentor.

Notice only the positive attitude is the one that makes impact. And that's why it's important to survey your responses to emotional triggers so you can get the insight into your attitude that you need to discover where it's leading you astray by skewing your perception. For this purpose, it might be wise to use a journal to record your self-assessments to review with objectivity. Be aware, though. Your greatest danger here is your ego. It can make you unconsciously maintain illusions about yourself that may be comforting in the moment, but in the long run make you defensive and unable to learn or progress. Sometimes temporal distance helps you find that point of objectivity and dims the voice of the ego. Or just setting the intention when you write about the incident in your journal that you will find a neutral position from which you can observe your actions with a bit of detachment and maybe even humor. Just making the effort to block out your ego will go a long way to funding success there.

FRAME YOUR STRENGTHS

Your strengths are one of the things that make you different from other people. As you'll discover in the Playbook, they are also guideposts for helping you decide which goals mesh with your long-term interests. When you combine that difference-making value with the aligning properties of your strengths, you get an awesome result: the ability to resist the pull of group bias that can affect your attitude.

By acknowledging that power, you can use it to deliberate longer before acting or to back your confidence as you reassess your strategies. Embracing your strengths will help your inner voice become clearer, so that when people besiege you with their endless dramas and petty emotions, you will resist the distractions and apply your rationality to think past them.

Like an athlete continually getting stronger through training, if you remain committed to allowing your strengths to come through and do their jobs, you will become more flexible and resilient. You will be clearer and calmer. You will see answers and creative solutions that no one else can envision.

In other words, you can learn to let your strengths, not your emotions, rule your attitude. The confidence that comes from knowing your strengths will help you approach people as allies and not as enemies to defend against. It will help you stay out of the zeitgeist of the moment, try new methods, and yes, be an explorer. In the end, your strengths can help you find, maintain, and utilize a blissful balance between your emotions and your attitude.

BLISSFUL BALANCE

Now you have a full understanding of what's going on inside you chemically that's fueling your emotions and how to build a foundation by controlling those emotions to make impactful actions. The thing is you don't need to be in acute stress all the time to make things happen.

In fact, when you're not under the influence of acute stressors (aka living a normal life) all those hormones and neurotransmitters are at a balanced state. That's when you have more space to think of the larger picture, to think of the greater good and expand on higher thought, and reorient yourself before another acute stressor strikes—just like that tiger beetle. That's the beauty of not being in survival mode. You can drop into your rest and digest system, you can now broaden your vision, and you have the ability to see a grander scale, so you can better handle whatever comes next.

As a student of impact, your job is to mimic that blissful balance as much as possible. That's why it's important to understand how those basic systems influence your ability to make positive or negative actions so you can actively work to reduce the negative effects.

You must also realize that you can't stop this phenomenon from happening in your body. You can only change how you respond to it. Higher-order functions like labeling feelings with words are just your mind's observation of the hormones released in your body and naming the emotions produced by them. But really, it's up to you to figure out how to translate that observation into actions in the real world. You must accept that reality and understand the impact it can have on you and those around you. Because negative actions thrive on ignorance, by taking this first step of self-observation, you can stop them at their source.

Another requirement as a student of impact is constantly practicing control over how your actions impact you. Remember, you need your stress chemicals in balance, and as we will discuss later, having a certain amount of stress in your life is incredibly important. It gives you energy, focus, and vision to achieve your goals. You need to practice the control of actions that can be negative to your big goals. That is, be aware of how you react, buy yourself some time to clear space, get a clearer head, and settle back into your bigger-picture thinking before going into action again.

To be clear, we are not saying you need to be a robot. We cannot divorce emotions from thinking. Those two are as intertwined as the tangled-up tinsel and lights you need to put on your Christmas tree. Actually, the ancient Greeks had an appropriate metaphor for this concept: the rider and the horse.

- The horse is our emotional nature, continually impelling us to move. The horse has tremendous energy and power, but without a rider it cannot be guided. It is wild, subject to predators, and continually heading into trouble.

- The rider is our thinking self. Through training and practice, the rider holds the reins and guides the horse, transforming the powerful animal energy into something productive.

One without the other is useless. Without the rider, no directed movement has purpose. Without the horse, there is no energy or power.

In some people, the horse dominates their actions and the rider is weak; the two wander aimlessly in various directions, never really making progress, constantly in a state of reaction. In others, the rider is too strong, holding the reins too tightly and afraid to occasionally let the animal go into a gallop.

The horse and rider must always work together. And we must always consider our actions beforehand; we must bring as much thinking as possible to a situation before we make a decision. Then, once we decide what to do, we can loosen the reins and enter action with boldness and a spirit of adventure.

Instead of being a slave to the energy within us, we can

choose to channel it. Be the horse and the rider. Seek to understand the forces behind your emotions and behavior so you can minimize their negative impacts and focus on maximizing and utilizing them for positive impact.

Use your energy when it drives you forward and no farther than that. And then be just a little Zen and use your logic when you need to make decisions.

Basically, it's like being an Australian tiger beetle: sprinting, then resting to reorient before sprinting and then resting to reorient before sprinting again...

Now that you have a clear idea of what it means to have a goal, you understand the anti-patterns behind your unimpactful actions, and you know how to handle your emotions so that you can make impactful actions, it's time to learn just what an impactful action is.

CHAPTER 5

IMPACTFUL ACTIONS

Two things create anxiety for most modern professionals. First, they don't understand how their performance is being evaluated. Second, they don't know if the actions they are taking, right now, are helping or hurting that evaluation.

The tension comes from the fact that they don't know if they are taking impactful actions—things you do to create value, or progress toward an overall goal, or unimpactful actions—things you do that create negative progress or value toward an overall goal.

All your actions fall into one of those two areas. There's no middle ground. (If you're taking an action that has a net-neutral impact, then you're wasting time that could have been spent on a positive one instead.) Since there are only a limited number of hours in a day you want to maximize the time you're spending on actions that have positive impact and minimize the actions that have negative impact.

The problem, however, is that most of us don't get feedback on our actions until significantly after the fact. We cruise along all year with a low-grade anxiety that we're doing the right work, but not sure how it's going to pan out, only to reach performance appraisal season, when our managers tell us that we got it all wrong and we're not getting a raise (again).

Wouldn't it be nice to not have wasted that time?

That answer to that question is the trick to joining the impact-making club: understanding which actions will be impactful before you take them, rather than spending time on them, only to realize the error of your ways too late.

We just spent the past few chapters talking about the types of actions that can create unimpactful actions. It was important to cover that first, since awareness of negative behaviors is the first step in correcting them. Hopefully, you've seen something there you'd like to address and can start fixing things up. Right now, though, it's time for us to talk about impactful actions: what they are, how you define them, and how you can keep doing them time and time again.

To start, we're going to finally get around to clearing up confusion about what "impact" is.

UNDERSTANDING IMPACT

Simply put, impact is a term used in corporations to represent the contribution of value that your actions created toward an end goal for stakeholders.

That sounds simple but there are a few aspects that need a little more drilling.

STAKEHOLDERS

Impact cannot exist without a stakeholder, group, or person in seniority that has a goal to which you're contributing. That is why impact is such a hard term to define; everyone has their own uniquely defined goals; thus, their definition of impact will be different too. But at the end of the day, impact cannot exist unless it's being done so for someone (which can be yourself).

This is an exceptionally important concept in the corporate arena. Your stakeholder defines what impact is. Equally important to remember: If you're working on multiple projects, each stakeholder will have a separate goal and thus a separate definition of what impact is, and those will change over time. Projects you worked on last year will have different stakeholders and different definitions of impact than projects you work on this year. This is why, when you ask ten people how to create impact, they give you ten different answers. It's all a matter of their perspective.

As far as your efforts for creating impact, that means you need to clearly know who the stakeholder is for your project or goal (even if it's just yourself) and how they are defining what value for that goal looks like. Doing so will allow you to walk into your performance evaluation with a clear sense of whom you've been doing work for and if they feel the work has added value to their goals.

MEASUREMENT

Impact only exists when it can be shown *how* you've contributed value toward an end goal. Or probably better stated: impact doesn't exist unless you can measure it.

Measuring your impact requires two things. First, you need to understand the baseline metrics that describe the progress of whatever the current goal is. Chances are, any goal or project you're contributing to isn't done in a vacuum, so there are other people and processes in place that are all contributing to it, and each person is trying to make their own impact. Because value is created based on the end goal, you need to understand what that value looks like, holistically, before you dive in. If you don't understand how many new users are downloading your company's app each day, you'll have no idea if your efforts changed that number at all, which brings us to the second point.

You need to be able to measure how *your actions* are influencing the metrics of the larger goal. If sending out daily email blasts increases app downloads, that's great. But if you can't definitively show that your emails caused the downloads to happen, then you've been basically wasting your time and you will not be able to prove you've had any impact.

Or perhaps more bluntly stated: If you're expecting the work you've done to land you that new promotion, you better be able to go to your manager with definitive evidence that your work contributed, strongly, to the end goals of the project. The more vague you are with this causal relationship, the harder it will be to prove that you've had impact.

This is, at its core, how to define impact: by understanding who is evaluating your work, what the baseline is, and how your efforts have created unique value toward it. One way I like to frame this is, "If they hadn't done this work, would the same result have happened?" For example, if app downloads were trending up by 4 percent month over month while Amy did nothing, we'd expect it to remain at 4 percent during evaluation time. If Amy did a whole bunch of work and claims to have influenced downloads, but the download rate hasn't moved from 4 percent, then it's unclear if her actions had any impact. However, if we can show that app downloads are now 8 percent and that the entirety of the 4 percent jump came from the efforts of Amy, then that's a great, clear sign of impact.

You don't need fancy databases and lots of engineering work to track your impact on a project. It can be as simple as understanding the bigger picture and what you contributed to it.

When hurricanes are imminent, humans often come together with the ultimate goal of aiding one another. That big goal is broken down into numerous sub-goals—some people help their neighbors pound plywood over vulnerable windows. Others volunteer to help set up shelters for those living in areas in need of evacuating. And still others set a goal of building a wall with a pile of sandbags along glass storefronts in downtown areas to keep the water outside the stores.

Aside from the big goal of saving the stores, the sandbag group has a smaller sub-goal of saving one store at a time. Within that goal are many sub-sub-goals, one for each bag of sand to get it from point A (the supply truck) to point B (the particular storefront).

Each person *could* carry the bag from the truck to the storefront, but that would be very tiresome for everyone, as the bags are quite heavy. Instead, a human supply chain is formed where people stand six feet apart, making a line from the truck to a storefront. They then hand the bags to one another, moving the sandbags six feet at a time until they are sufficiently stacked in front of the window.

Each person in the chain is contributing to the end goal of preventing the storefront from flooding. They could each say their impact was six feet for each bag of sand. For their total impact on the project, they could multiply that by however many bags of sand they helped transport. They could also weigh the bags and know how many pounds they moved as their impact.

A SIMPLE EXAMPLE

Say you own a new start-up and that you've set your company goal to double revenue this year in order to sock some cash into savings to support the expected growth next year. "Double revenue" is the stated goal, so you know where you are heading. It also satisfies the deed to create a baseline, which is where your revenue is now. Now it's just a matter of doing Step 3: take action to double revenue.

You refine your goal a bit more by deciding you want to double revenue through an effective use of marketing. You then create various ad campaigns and measure their effectiveness on increasing revenue. The ad campaigns are your Step 3 because you can measure their impact on your income.

It's easier to set your own goals and figure out which actions you'll measure to reach them. But for many of us, those goals are set for us by our supervisors or team leads and we're left semi-clueless about what to do to make impact. We'll carry on with the double-revenue theme to help here, since it's a favorite among CEOs. It's big. It's bold. But most importantly, it's vague—so they can use it as a directive but are not responsible for how it's done.

In such cases, it's very unclear what specific actions you, either as a direct report or as a member of a group, need to take to make impact on that goal. You could do it by creating a new product or service. You could do it by improving the quality of an existing product. You could do it by increasing marketing spend or sales team size or by connecting with key influencers. There would most likely be numerous possibilities.

However, whether it's you or a team lead, someone will make a choice. Hopefully, they will narrow the choice down as much as possible. Something like "our goal is to double revenue in the Japan market by bringing in new customers" would be just fine. You, though, will need to figure out what your part of that overall goal is and define it in a way you can measure it. Then define your actions in a way that can be measured too. Maybe your contribution to bringing in customers from the Japan market is to sign on fifty sushi restaurants to use your DIY ordering software. If revenue doubled and you only signed thirty restaurants, your actions had a greater impact than planned—praise 'n' raise for you.

An important concept to keep in mind regarding measuring impact is that sometimes you will be given a goal with a deadline that comes long after your performance appraisal. In some cases, like for a new product expected to be released in two years, you may even have a few performance appraisals between the time you were given the goal and the time it was reached. These three steps still apply in that case. You *must* always be able to prove what you have done, that is, what you have contributed to a goal whether it's reached or not. That is an important mental model to get because it helps define and frame what impactful actions look like: actions that result in a measurable contribution toward the goal.

To determine how well an action is helping you make that

contribution, you need to know how to measure the quality of that action.

In mathematics, a vector is something that helps us determine where a point in space is relative to another point in space. It is usually depicted as an arrow, the length of which is the magnitude of the vector, and an arrow pointing on one end is the direction the vector is going. Math vectors can go in any direction in two-dimensional or three-dimensional space. These kinds of vectors often torment linear algebra students in college and are vital for the creation of things like video games, computer-rendered movies, and 3-D printing.

Perhaps not to be outdone by the math majors, biologists have their own spin on vectors. In their world, a vector is an organism that a host carries from one thing to another. A prime example of this kind of vector is the anopheles mosquito. When it bites a person infected with malaria, it doesn't get sick with the disease. Instead, it acts as a vector and allows the parasite to travel via "Air Mosquito" until it lands on another mammal. At that point, perhaps feeling cramped in the tiny insect salivary glands where the legroom is ridiculously small, the parasite bids adieu to its host and subsequently infects something else with malaria.

While neither definition of a vector sounds like a particularly good time, there is something common to both that is important here when we talk about impact. Whether in math or in biology, *vector refers to movement,* that is action, toward an endpoint—a goal. So to look at your goal and your impact in terms of vectors, you can see:

The stated goal is the point of origin for your vector; the arrow points in the direction of the goal, which is the endpoint of the vector.

The length of your vector already in place is your baseline.

Your impact, then, is the change in the vector length that you create with the new actions you take.

IMPACTFUL ACTIONS

The whole point of our process is to be able *before the fact* to understand what actions we can take that will produce impact, rather than learning all too late that we've been wasting our time. This is the Zen of achieving our goals and getting the rewards that come with it. To do this, we need to be able to evaluate whether a given action is impactful or not.

There are three aspects of an action that determine the quality of it: the outcome you derive from it; the energy that goes into making it; and the ejecta, the side effects and potential collateral damage that is kicked up after the impact happens. Certain sports, like golf, provide excellent visual examples of each one. When a golf club hits a golf ball, the outcome is the ball is sent sailing (or rolling, if the club was a putter). You can measure the force of the swing, which is the energy, and outcome, which is how far the ball goes. And the ejecta is whatever sand is kicked up, if the shot goes astray into a pit, or a bruise on a bystander's forehead, if it goes even further astray.

In order for the golf swing to be an impactful one for our definitions, the right amount of force was used, the ball went in the direction and length desired to land on the green, and no one was hurt. *Clearly, impactful actions need to be done with precision, intention, and with an understanding of potential collateral damage.* We must spend a great deal of time honing our ability to execute actions accordingly.

However, there's a catch. It's easy to get tunnel vision and focus exclusively on *how* to execute the actions correctly. By doing that we risk losing sight of the end results, our goals, or reasoning behind the actions. The danger in doing that is we can stall out our careers by getting stuck on an action. We see this in engineers who are excited by a new programming language, so they spend all their time and energy rewriting code for that language, when in reality, it changes nothing for their team's goal. It has no real impact.

Similar situations happen with creatives. A new trend comes out that captures the heart and creative drive of someone and they start seeing the world entirely through the lens of that trend. They choose actions to satisfy their creative drive without realizing they are shifting their goal to something that's immeasurable: taking this action to support the trend. They then lose traction in their career because they are too focused on doing work that inspires them, instead of work that creates impact. And this explains why the world is periodically flooded with unicorn images.

Granted, taking an action conflates with the creation of impact. But while those things can be causal in relationship, it's easy to see how they can also separate from each other. If you choose the wrong actions to take or you spend too much time focusing on execution or if the actions you're taking produce *unintended* results, then they are not impactful actions. We must always remember: Actions are not themselves valuable; impact is.

And impactful actions create a positive change in a measurable outcome on a goal, while minimizing effort and side effects.

THE OUTCOME

Many moons ago, when I was a younger human, I had a kickboxing instructor who had a favorite phrase: "Would you start a fistfight if you knew you were going to lose?"

His point was to help us understand that you shouldn't engage in certain activities if the outcome was unsure, or net negative. I mean, you can think you're the fiercest person in the bar, but as soon as you mouth off to the person missing a nose, you might get your worldview corrected.

In the corporate world, the same mentality applies: Actions create outcomes. So before we run off and spend time and energy on those actions, we should know what we're expecting from the effort. And there are two ways of figuring that out:

- On the front side, we have to make sure that we have enough visibility into the action and what we expect the output to be. That will enable us to make a sensible deduction that our actions will, in fact, lead to a specific result. This means doing your homework and running the right types of tests to gain insight.

- On the back side, we need to make sure that we are measuring the outcomes, so that during our performance reviews later we can clearly define that our actions did, in fact, have impact.

The main concept here is that for actions you take, you should have an expectation of what the expected output is and an expectation of how to measure it for proof later. If you ignore either of those two (taking an action without knowing the outcome or not measuring it) then, by definition, it's unimpactful.

That being said, there are some grey areas here. For example, there's going to be a whole boatload of actions you need to take that don't have dashboard-ready measurable metrics. If getting approval for a project means improving relationships with a cross-functional team, you might have to put in a lot of work in a lot of small tasks to produce that final immeasurable goal.

At other times, there will be plenty to measure but you can't do so directly. Like deep-space researchers trying to find exo-planets. They can't directly see the planets so instead, they measure how a star slightly shifts in the night sky, signaling that there might be a planet large enough to assert its gravitational effect on the star. Since they can't see the thing they want directly, they have to create a proxy metric that alludes to its existence. We spoke about this concept earlier: it is operationalization, and it will be the cornerstone of your efforts as you attempt to measure the unmeasurable.

The key to operationalization is to choose terms and metrics that everyone will agree means some specific thing and then document the hell out of it, so no one forgets. Later, as you go through to prove the value of your actions, you'll be able to rely on a clear measurable term, instead of a vague one that no one agrees on.

The key to impact, then, is making sure that someone cares about the metric you're measuring. It has to have value to someone to be considered impactful. This is critical to keep in mind as you're going through your process of understanding your outcomes. Ask yourself, "Will I be able to show that this outcome matters in some measurable way to someone who cares?" If you can, then your action will be impactful.

Keep the deep-space analogy in mind as you go about your professional and even personal lives. You will not always be able to take actions where the impact is measurable in clearly defined increments, like a run scored in baseball. Sometimes you will take a set of actions, like an ice skater, where you're being judged based on a loose framework.

That framework can change day to day or from person to person, so it's a good idea to know what is expected of you as much as you can. Otherwise, you may end up wasting a lot of energy, which, as we're about to see, is what makes your actions create impact.

THE ENERGY

We have to understand that each action has a certain amount of resources that need to be sacrificed for it to be accomplished—and create measurable impact. For the purposes of this book, we're calling those resources *energy*.

Energy can be hours, money, time, or people. It could be the mental resources required to solve complex problems. It could be the stain remover sticks you keep stocked in your desk drawer to ensure the salsa blob that dripped from your breakfast burrito is no longer visible when you greet your clients.

As you're evaluating the tasks required for you to create impact, you'll want to define what type of energy each action will take. While there's a large swath of options, most of them fall into:

- Time: how long will it take?
- Money: what does it cost for the people or processes involved?

- People: how many humans are required for this task?
- Political coin: what kind of relationships do you need to tap into?
- Physiological energy: the amount of stress, late nights, or time in an unsafe scenario you may need to engage in.

When we consider the energy required for an action, we're looking at the factors involved to determine if there are trade-offs that would be beneficial. For example, it might take twelve months to build a prototype. That energy spent is in the form of time, which may be a precious commodity when you need to do the task. In that case, you look to see if there is a trade-off. Perhaps you can pay a vendor $300,000 who can build it in three months. That 300K is cheaper than the additional payroll the project would require, and that would free up some of the team members to focus on other projects.

At a more personal level, let's look at a job search. When you're looking for a job, you have a variety of tasks to do. You can spend the time and political coin networking or you can go to a recruiting agency who is paid by companies to find the right people for them. You have to figure out which is the best investment of your energy to have the most impact. If you're loaded with cash but short on time, perhaps the recruiter is the right way to go. However, if you're short on cash and long on time, using your political coin might be in your best interest.

An object in motion will stay in motion until a force acts upon it.

—ISAAC NEWTON

Something to remember when you're considering the trade-offs for your energy: if your action intends to disrupt the status quo, expect to expend, on average, three times the amount of energy than you would to maintain or follow it.

And the more disruption you have, the more *ejecta*. Ejecta is the collateral damage that kicks up from actions and is one of the things that helps determine how impactful your actions are.

THE EJECTA

Words are like arrows. Once loosed, you cannot call them back.

—GEORGE R. R. MARTIN

Newton's Laws of Motion, specifically the third law, which states that "for each action, there is an equal and opposite reaction," is perhaps most apt when we discuss ejecta from our impact, and a comet is most apt to create a good visual for it.

When a comet slams into a planet—hopefully not Earth—the impact of it kicks up quite a bit of debris. Rocks and dirt knocked out of the way by the energy of the comet's force fly about and create impacts of their own as they land on whatever it is they land on.

The comet is a clear example of how impact in the physical sense usually results in dispersed energy distribution. The volumes of rock and dirt, the ejecta, is often an overlooked phenomenon. Though it can be one of the reasons your actions are determined impactful or unimpactful.

We have to remind ourselves that when we take impactful actions there will always be side effects (ejecta) that come with it. If your goal is to have more money in your bank account, one action you could take is to rob your rich uncle Harold. However, the side effects would be either living your life as a hermit or being caught and doing time in prison because everyone knows Uncle Harold holds a grudge. The size, quantity, and quality of the ejecta all determine whether actions are impactful or unimpactful.

Some actions can produce very little, if any, side effects. For example, switching vendors that provide your materials at a cheaper price may have very little ejecta, given that the terms are similar—unless your prior vendor is vindictive and begins spreading vicious rumors about your company. Meanwhile, others can produce massive, problematic side effects. You may hit a very difficult, impossible deadline while pushing your coworkers to the edge of their sanity. Sure, the work got completed, but once it's over, you now have an angry mob with whom you've destroyed your relationships.

Perhaps one of the most well-known examples of the power of ejecta is the story behind why Steve Jobs was removed from the company he'd founded due to how he went about accomplishing impact.

Jobs had a reputation for being difficult to work with, for pushing people to hit impossible deadlines, and for having no sense of empathy. Things came to a head in 1985 when Apple released the Lisa, the first computer with a graphical user interface (GUI). It was Jobs' baby—he'd pushed for it; he was the one who wanted it out on the market. While it was deemed a technical marvel, no one wanted to buy it. The market wasn't ready. Sales were almost nonexistent.

Undaunted, Jobs pushed the Macintosh, which sold better but not good enough to stake a hold in the PC market. Long story short, he was reassigned and then, after all his pushing of others and products, he himself was pushed out of the company. Granted, there are those who say he resigned; he claimed he was fired.

Regardless of the final verdict, the core lesson was clear: Sure, he was a genius with amazing ideas for world-impacting products and technologies. But he had the reputation of a hothead who was unconcerned about the well-being of those around him. That disregard for his teams, coworkers, and ultimately the board that he reported to, created a huge swath of ejecta, which piled up significantly after not being dealt with over time. The result then, was his removal from his position.

Because of this, it's important to remember that impact is not the end; it's the middle. Once impact occurs, you have to deal with each of the ejecta, the impact of which will create more ejecta, etc.

We started this discussion on ejecta by bringing up Newton's third law. But his second law also applies here: Every action has an equal and opposite reaction. Every time you create ejecta, you have a new action—just like with the debris that scatters after a comet's impact. You end up in this spot where you are always moving half the distance to the goal. That means you want to be sure you're always cleaning up the debris you create, or it will just clutter up your path to your goal.

Yes, this creates an endless cycle of doing work that creates side effects that create work that creates side effects, and on and on and on. When you create your Playbook, you'll learn how to predict the kind of ejecta you can expect and how to clean it up, so it doesn't cause you more work than is really necessary to reach your goal. It's critical that as you're planning and choosing impactful actions, that you're planning beyond the impact event through the clearing of ejecta from your playing field.

All actions, regardless of their intention, have side effects. When we're searching for the right types of impactful actions to take, we must properly compare the impact and effort against the ejecta. What actions we choose can ebb and flow depending on how those values change. If given the choice between two actions that produce similar impact, we might choose the one with more ejecta due to the fact it requires less effort.

In fact, some problems are so big, that all the side effects of solutions yield a stalemate in taking any action at all.

The ability to quantify measure, your impact is the only way you'll know whether your efforts and actions are doing what they are supposed to do: hit the goal. And they are the only way of knowing whether you earned the plush cubicle.

GET SOME CONTEXT: STORYTIME WITH COLT

Mac left a job with a gaming company where he created tools to measure performance graphics and went to work for a larger corporation, for which games were a minor part, pretty much doing the same thing. While he was impressed with much of what the new company was doing, he couldn't help but be surprised by a few things that he thought they could do better, and he didn't keep his opinions to himself.

"Hey, you know, these tools should be better," he'd freely tell people in passing. "In the games industry they do a better job with tools." On and on his criticism went for the team, which was developing the things he felt were subpar.

Eventually, his nonstop negativity came to a head. He was called into a meeting with the manager of the team and the HR rep for his team. In essence, and in not-so-polite words, Mac was told to be a little more discrete with his critical opinions and to just focus on his job.

Perhaps we should let you know here that he was very young and inexperienced in the ways of office politics. He said, "fine," and left. But he wasn't done.

In fact, Mac created an external campaign where he did very public talks to large groups of people. He spoke about the performance of webpages. At each one, he'd mention that he was limited in what he could teach. "I wish I could tell you that this was a problem and show it to you in the tools," he'd say. "But the tools do not have that ability. However, if you'd like them to, you can click this link." The link, of course, would send a request for the tools to the manager who had asked him to please stop being so critical.

After about eight weeks, Mac was called back into a room with the manager of the team he'd disparaged, his own manager, and the HR rep for his team.

This meeting started off on a pleasant foot. They thanked Mac for his efforts. "You've created more blogs, more posts, and more conference talks than anyone else. Your conference attendance is through the roof. Our Twitter followers have quadrupled. So, thank you." They gave him a bonus and Mac was happy.

But they weren't done. "That being said," his manager continued, "you can't work on this team anymore. While we thank you for highlighting our deficiencies and helping us see that developers around the world want those tools, none of us appreciates the way that you did this. And we felt that you were being extremely aggressive and intentionally harmful. You have thirty days to find another job."

Clearly Mac took action to create a change, but the ejecta of losing his job suggests it was unimpactful action.

OUTCOMES, ENERGY, EJECTA, OH MY!

There once was a suburban homeowner who liked to walk his dogs around the neighborhood in the evening. Once, the dogs needed to stop and water a lawn they'd never been past. Suddenly, an irate elderly homeowner bounced up from his porch to yell at the man and tell him to keep the dogs off his lawn. The outburst caught the man off guard, but he took a breath and asked the senior citizen why he was yelling at him.

"Those dogs are killing my grass!" he proclaimed, followed by a tirade of insults and comments about the respect of the community he lived in. The man thanked him for his perspective and moved along with his dogs. Later, he considered the situation with a little more perspective. The retired gentlemen had an impact problem. What was his goal? To keep his front lawn healthy but dog urine was killing it. How was he going about achieving that goal? Sitting on his porch and angrily yelling at people as they walked by. What was the ejecta? He was probably not going to win any popularity contests any time soon.

The dog walker considered the situation a bit more. The old man's efforts seemed completely off. He can't sit on his porch all day and yell at everyone who walks by. Eventually, he'd need to eat or sleep, meaning there'd be windows where he'd miss yelling at people. Likewise, doing daily walks for a number of years, the dog walker had never encountered the man, so either his love of his lawn was a new development, or they'd just never been in the vicinity of each other at the same time. So the older man's effort was clearly achieving some part of his goal and he was probably loving having a chance to yell at people and feel superior but could he be more impactful?

Time and anger seemed to be in abundance for this gentleman, so what other options were available as a trade-off?

Building a fence around his yard would decrease the dog urine by 100 percent and would also mean he would no longer need to dedicate his time to patrolling the yard. Sadly, fences cost money (resources) and in some neighborhoods, can decrease your home value (ejecta). There are cheaper fencing options (temporary fencing, for example) but they decrease curb appeal even more, and you couldn't just assume the gentleman had those resources.

In a similar vein, the ejecta could be reduced by replacing the grass with a variety that is more resistant to dog urine. But again, that would be spending a lot of money to dig up a lawn, which, besides a few areas, seemed to be fine. You couldn't assume that the time and energy trade-off would be worth it.

That leaves: how do you dissuade folks from allowing their dogs to visit the lawn, at a low cost, and with low attention? A small, inexpensive sign might work. It would have the ability to guard the yard in the absence of the gentleman and hopefully there'd be fewer cases of bad actors ignoring the sign. Signs are cheap, which would fix our issue of resources. But if left to the older gentleman's decisions, it might say something inappropriate (ejecta). But it would be low cost, low energy, and if he picked the right phrase, low ejecta for the dog owner.

The dog owner set off to the hardware store and produced three signs at twenty-four inches tall—just the right height that any dog owner would have to manage the logistics of their dog around the signs and thus couldn't avoid them. On each sign he wrote, "Grass is healing, please no dogs for the summer." It was a gentle phrase that (hopefully) would lean on the shared suburban strife of keeping your lawn in order.

A little after dusk, the dog owner visited the lawn in question, placed the signs, and scurried back home. Much to his joy, the signs remained at the edge of the yard for weeks—apparently, the homeowner thought they were valuable—and during that time, the grass, did indeed recover. Even though it was never discussed, at the end of the summer, the signs went down and the lawn was doing fine.

This story points to how all three of these parts of impact have to come together. You have to consider the parts of impact, energy, and ejecta when deciding your actions and then test them appropriately based upon your context. Trying to evaluate any single one will mean you're missing an opportunity.

Since impactful action is our framework for forward-looking observation, planning, and execution, and yet we're constantly at the mercy of reacting, it's important to understand how to change poor reactions into impactful reactions.

CHAPTER 6

IMPACTFUL REACTIONS

The trick with evaluating what the potential outcome, energy, and side effects of an action could be, is that it takes time to do so. You have to sit (or walk) and think deeply about strategy components, options, what or who might be involved in the aftermath, and more. Perhaps if you always had enough time and enough resources, you would always make a perfect decision, take the perfect actions, and achieve perfect impact. Sadly, as with most things when superlatives like "always" and "perfect" are used, that's a pipe dream. What's a reality, though, is that we usually lack the time or resources—and sometimes both—needed for that research.

Think about how frequently you are bombarded with requests for action. Emails, text pings, and people stopping you in the hallway on your way to see if any bagels are left in the breakroom often interrupt your normal thought processes to ask you to do something—i.e., take an action—on their behalf and they want an immediate, or at least an ASAP, response.

With no time or resources to reflect on the request, you respond by reacting, which is seldom a good idea. Reactions, by definition, are a response to an immediate stimulus. So when we react, it's generally from a vulnerable vantage point; one from where our actions easily create a negative impact on our true goal. You stub your toe and reactively curse while your child is watching. That's a negative impact on your goal of raising well-behaved children because now your kid will be swearing on the playground in front of his kindergarten teacher when he stubs his toe.

Your coworker kicks in your door and starts yelling about how they didn't like your tone in an email—that's a reaction.

Your partner asks you a leading question that elicits an emotional response from you—that's a reaction.

When you get that request in the hallway and do not have time for an ASAP response but instead may take action before you get the bagel, you'll take action from a hangry point of view—that's a reaction.

On the other side, though, is what makes impactful actions work: time to do the proper planning and strategy creation.

But because sudden events sometimes occur that do not give us the time to plan and evaluate in the right state of mind, we need to find a way *not* to reflexively react and potentially create negative impact.

While there are hundreds of ways to deal with these situations, I've found a few tried-and-true generalizations you should keep in mind as you go through your day-to-day life.

UNMET EXPECTATIONS

Follow your heart but take your brain with you.

—ALFRED ADLER

Predominantly, the reason reactions have the potential to be problematic is that they interrupt our expectations. We may not always acknowledge it, but we have expectations for everything. We squeeze a tube and expect toothpaste to exit it. We click on an app and expect it to open, then we expect it to perform in a certain way.

When we think and plan or engage in a work process, there is a cadence and output we expect to happen. When someone else interrupts or prevents our expectations from being met, well, that's just asking for trouble. As any good counselor will tell you, anger is an emotional response to an unfulfilled expectation. Thus, when we react to interruptions it is easy to do so out of anger or frustration.

Interestingly, sometimes we're angry or frustrated simply because we didn't expect to be in a reactionary state, yet that's precisely where we are.

As we discussed earlier, anger is not the kind of emotion that makes for easy conversations and agreements to happen. The chemical dump we experience when angered, narrows our vision, mental scope, and puts our worldview in a perspective of survival instead of collaboration. In other words, when our expectations are not met, it leaves us in a poor place for problem-solving.

A good way to compound anger reactions is to have two people simultaneously be prevented from their expectations being realized. Many people experienced that kind of situation throughout 2020 when, while working at home, they expected their work time to be uninterrupted, meanwhile their children expected their parents to be at their beck and call. When those two expectations clashed, emotions frequently ran high and often a bottle (wine or milk) wound up being a resource in the peace-making-process.

To protect your relationships (not to mention your liver), you need to learn how to manage unmet expectations in a way that allows you to make impactful actions. Frequently, that's simply a matter of expecting to have them—yes, expect your expectations not to be met. By doing so, you can plan ahead of time for how to handle those situations.

For example, if you expect to be interrupted by pings and texts while focusing on analyzing data for a project, then you have a few options for dealing with them. One is to arrange your day to give yourself plenty of time to respond without feeling rattled. There's nothing like the stress of a fast-approaching deadline to amp up your expectations to be left alone to do your work. If that's not an option, then you need to arrange your environment to make yourself periodically unavailable. Maybe that means putting your phone in airplane mode for a couple of hours or possibly working at that café down the street that brags about not having Wi-Fi.

So as you can see, by anticipating that your expectations may not be met, you can plan ahead for whatever may hinder your progress. By doing so, you put yourself in a better frame of mind when it comes time to respond, which puts mental resources at the ready to think through your response.

However, we cannot anticipate and therefore plan, around all potential interruptions that can come our way. So we need to back up that strategy for using time and space to provide a buffer for you and, instead, create some mental and emotional buffers for yourself. And you do that through empathetic communication.

Once I took a wilderness survival course from a renown bush-master. He commented that he frequently gets requests from TV producers who want great survival-against-all-odds stories. He always disappoints them because he has none, which confuses the producers. They are under the impression that if you're running a survival school, surely you must have some outrageous survival tales to tell.

"Survival hinges more around being prepared then being in the moment," he tells them. "By planning ahead, understanding how situations might turn south, and preparing properly, I've avoided getting myself into those positions. Better yet, I've been in a number of spots to help out those who did get caught in bad places."

See, behind every ping, text, call, or tap on the shoulder, there is someone with expectations of their own, expectations that somehow involve you. When you can figure out what their expectations are, it's easier to see how their communication with you isn't wholeheartedly negative, vindictive, incendiary, or aggressive; it's just them trying to rectify their own expectations against an ever-changing world, and you're in the direct path of that.

This idea takes considerable time to master, but at its core, this is the cornerstone of empathetic communication. You develop the ability to forgo reacting negatively to a situation, even when someone is playing the role of an aggressor, because you understand that their actions aren't about you, it's about them and something they are dealing with. So when Todd sends you an email in all caps asking why it's so hard for you to write the proper code on time, instead of reacting by replying in all caps BECAUSE YOU DIDN'T GIVE ME DECENT PARAMETERS, YOU IDIOT, you'll realize he's upset with himself and worried he may have messed things up. You'll understand he was really yelling at himself and the situation and pleading with you for help.

> A common element behind so much strife and conflict in a workplace are the intersections created by multiple people with their own expectations all interacting, interrupting, and reacting to one another. If just one of those folks allows themself to have a negative reaction, a whole negative reactionary chain can be set off. Your goal is to avoid being that person.

Another way of looking at empathetic communication is that you're really learning how not to take things personally. And yes, that's hard to do and takes a considerable amount of time to master. However, it is possible and made easier when you can figure out what the expectations of others are, which brings us to the second tool for learning to control your reactions: observe and understand.

OBSERVE AND UNDERSTAND

At the core of being able to take impactful actions is the concept of having the full picture of a situation—or at least as much of the full picture as possible. To do that means you take the time to think, explore, and understand as much about your goals as you can, so that you will learn how to operate in that space and know where your boundaries are.

When we allow ourselves to react with knee-jerk emotional responses, it's usually because we do not have that full picture. So we find ourselves being put "on the spot" to make decisions or being given new information about our efforts from seemingly out of the blue. When either happens, we run the risk of responding emotionally and giving incorrect answers that are based on only part of the larger narrative.

So before we react, we must see how the new information fits into our holistic worldview and what ramifications that may have for our plans. That's the observe part of this tool. The understand part is a little more difficult.

Understanding requires you to survey the mental model of your goal and the world around you to make sure you've got things right. This doesn't apply just to when people interrupt you or your expectations aren't met by others—it's not unusual to stumble across an unknown variable that we hadn't planned for as we make strides toward our goals. Similar to being interrupted or others failing to meet our expectations, when this happens, confusion and unimpactful actions can occur due to our own misunderstandings. So as we receive new information, or when we're put into a position of reaction, we need to *first figure out if we've got things wrong* before taking an action. This is a critical step for collaboration and communication. If your first reaction is simply to defend your position, worldview, or ideas as inherently correct, then you run the risk of causing more strife than progress. You have to step back and question your own model and make sure you're thinking about things the right way or is it possible you could be wrong about something? Could someone else have a better idea?

Once we let ourselves accept that we might not always have the one right answer, we need to reflect on the new information and the situations behind it as deeply as possible so that we fully understand it. When people bring you new information, it's likely just the tip of the iceberg; you'll only see a small part of the bigger worldview that they have in their mind. If you react simply on that information, then you run the risk of limiting your options.

For example, let's say you are creating a process to streamline a convoluted file-retrieval system, and someone interrupts you to tell you "in my old job, we used this tool," and they name a program. It happens to be a program that you dismissed earlier as not being sophisticated enough and you're annoyed that they interrupted you, so you wave them off and give a curt "thanks but no thanks," response. What you could be missing out on is how that person's previous employer used that program with a particular add-on that is now doing precisely what you're spending quite a bit of mental anguish trying to figure out.

So when receiving new information, you need to unearth what isn't being said before you can evaluate what HAS been said. This is where the technique of the five whys comes into play: by asking "why" at least five times, you can help unearth a lot of extra data about the situation, which might otherwise be hidden due to emotion, confusion, or mismatched priorities.

Once you've absorbed the new information, you then have to modify your actions, plans, and worldview accordingly. Sometimes new information might be incorrect, though, and not require you to adjust. But you won't know unless you acquired a full picture, understood it completely, and then evaluated the outcome of a change in strategy—i.e., weighed it against ejecta.

In short, the trick to making your reactions impactful actions is to stop, observe, and absorb new information properly.

MASTER TIME AND SPACE

Space I can recover, lost time never.

—NAPOLEON BONAPARTE

Impactful reactions are challenging because, by definition, they are expecting you to take an action within a certain timeframe. This varies by medium: You might be able to put off an email for a couple days, but someone stopping you in the hallway demands an answer—now. The more physical the interaction, the more the other person expects an urgent response.

Urgency is something that short-circuits our emotional safeguards by, again, causing emotional reactions. Marketing and sales tactics are designed to force a sense of urgency in you, so that your fear of missed opportunity overrides your sense of "not spending too much money this month," and that comes down to tapping into the human state of loss aversion.

When we are placed into a reactive state, time is a very valuable commodity. It takes time to survey our mental model, ask questions, absorb new information, and then figure out how this affects our plans and what actions we need to take as a result. This understanding of the role time plays in decision-making and action taking is critical for your perspective. Unless you're a medical professional, athlete, or a live performer, chances are that very few actions in your life must be decided within a millisecond of time. Instead, understand that the urgency that might be coming with the requests is just an illusion, something you can bend and warp to your needs: if no one is going to die within the next ten minutes, then surely you can ask for a few hours before giving a response?

That is our final trick to impactful reactions: mastering the ability to create space for the situation and create the time to understand and absorb it.

Stanford's School of Design curriculum uses a book called *Make Space: How to Set the Stage for Creative Collaboration* by Scott Doorley, Scott Witthoft, et al, that discusses the spaces humans need in a business environment. They've identified that we need a place—like an auditorium—where leadership can address the team. We also need a space where relaxed communication can occur. We need quiet spaces for dedicated focus work. And we need pressure-release spaces where people can get together and socialize.

Despite being designated spaces for specific purposes, these spaces attract clutter. If you don't have a dedicated space for something, or you have something that doesn't fit into the dedicated space, then it just stays in this awkward position. The authors recommended having a dedicated space to place things that don't fit anywhere else right now, and if at the end of a certain time period, let's say a month, you haven't figured out where that thing goes yet, you either need to just move it or throw it away. It's the equivalent of the junk drawer in your kitchen.

We can look at our inbound work system in a similar way. By employing purposeful procrastination, we can move tasks or demands from other people that they insist we need to focus on immediately to a place where we can look at them with a better perspective.

For example, when something comes to you that you're not in a frame of mind to deal with without it causing you stress, you can respond with, "I'm going to put it in this bucket over here until I get more data on it." That's a more gracious way of accepting it without forcing yourself to do something that red-hot minute rather than pushing back immediately with irritation or even aggression. Then, after giving yourself some space and time, you may be in a better place mentally and emotionally to respond, ask for help, or do whatever was asked of you. By giving yourself that mental space, you are creating the ability to triage it more accurately.

This process of making space for your inbound work is critical in understanding how to manage your time for these events. It forces you to put time and distance between the ingestion of information and reacting to it. The longer you can resist reacting, the more mental space you have for actual reflection and perspective. It also lets any emotional triggers filter through your body, so you can think more clearly, and your mind becomes stronger.

Using this strategy makes time your friend. A little space, a little distance, a little time to process can save you years of negative impact and side effects.

NO TIME? TRUST YOUR GUT

Now that being said, we have to always adhere to any non-movable timeframes. If you've got thirty seconds to defuse a bomb, chances are you can't ask for an extension on time. If your boss expects your report by Wednesday, so it can be presented to the director on Friday, then chances are, you can't move those meetings. If a coworker is blocked on something, then it might make more sense to handle their challenges now rather than seven days later. As such, we need to be able to gain ourselves as much time as possible, but when the jig is up, we must be okay with the results we present.

While we point out that the trick to impactful actions relies on planning and understanding, we have to realize that the more you do it, the more context you'll have in a space, the more experience you'll have within that space, hence the better you will be at making decisions in that space. This is intrinsically what we call having a feel for things that are impactful or not. This is how pro athletes make microsecond decisions based upon a flood of information—they've seen a scenario so many times, their brains are able to extrapolate and apply a cost/risk framework without the rest of their cognitive mind realizing what's going on. This is also why your company just hired a new VP with a crazy number of zeros in their salary: they are expecting that background and history of decisions and experience to allow them to make a quick impact on the bottom line.

As such, when placed under time constraints, you either have the experience to trust your gut, or you don't. If you're not there yet, then do your best to elevate the decision (reaction) to someone who might have that experience. Most likely, you're surrounded by coworkers who've seen or heard something similar to the problem you're encountering. Asking them for quick advice might be the key to success. Doing this repeatedly will give you a mental bucket of patterns and experiences that you can recall later on. When a new situation doesn't fit your existing mental model, you can find a previous situation that was "close enough" and use that as a basis for decision-making. Doing this over-and-over again is what builds your ability to react in a positive way, make decisions, and create impact in a short timeframe.

At the end of the day, reactions are inevitable; you will always be in a situation where you're reacting. The more planning you've done, the more gut feel you will develop and your situation will allow you to subconsciously make decisions toward your end goal without even thinking about it. You'll be able to trust your decision-making process because you've seen it enough times.

Once you've reached that level, then you are truly a student of impact and you're ready to build your own Impactful Actions Playbook. That's where you will put together your own resource for impactful actions. You'll start by learning how to develop adaptive strategies to plan better for reaching your goals in a complex world. Then you'll become an oracle of sorts—you'll master the ability to predict which actions will have the best outcomes. You will also find new ways to tap into resources for potential actions by researching and reaching out to others. Once you've gathered an assortment of actions, you'll label them and then you'll be ready to execute. It might sound like a lot to do, but really, it's like walking down the street—just start out and go one step at a time.

PART III!

MAKE A PLAN

CHAPTER 7

IMPACTFUL ACTIONS PLAYBOOK

Now that you know how to choose a clear, measurable goal and you know what an impactful action looks like, it's time to combine those two concepts and figure out how to make an impactful action toward your goal or, rather, make impactful actions. As you might have already figured out, big goals require multiple steps and often a long period of time to reach them. If you've ever volunteered to make a run to the food vendors at a music festival, you might already know how this feels. It takes a lot of right choices to leave your friends; find and purchase orange chicken burritos, grilled shrimp kebabs, pulled pork sandwiches, fried Oreos, and the *correct* ginger beer; and then safely return to them with loaded arms before your favorite band starts.

Whether your deadline is a headlining artist or the on-sale

date of a new product your team is creating, time is passing. And that means there is always potential for things to change. If there's a shift in the market, your company may cut its budget. If your competitor brings out an almost identical app before you do, you may need to change your offerings. And if the third food tent doesn't have fried Oreos, you might have to experiment a little with candied bacon. The key point is that time will always change the operating parameters of your goals. Because of that, you cannot only rely on a particular set of actions. Instead, you need to build a system or a framework with which you can collect potential actions and manage them so you can shift or modify them according to changes in the context around you. We call such a system a *playbook*. When used correctly, it can be the difference between continuing to take impactful actions or falling off the path into the unknown.

Once properly built, your playbook will be able to get you through the complex systems of work and life to make impact on your goals. You'll be able to create adaptive strategies to handle the unexpected and you'll discover how to source potential actions, label them, and then execute them.

ADAPTIVE STRATEGIES

As you start to practice the techniques we've discussed in this book, you'll eventually start seeing your ability to make impact start to rise. You will start seeing things clearer, understand the systems and how they are related better, and be able to identify what is going to waste your time before you...well, waste your time on it. Once you start gaining this type of traction, you should be delighted. Success is nigh! Revel in your progress. But do so with the knowledge that you may fall into a large trap: assuming the patterns and actions you've found will work in every situation.

We've all seen that manifest dozens of times. Someone works with a mentor and soon begins realizing explosive growth, success, and impact. They're in the groove, strutting along like Harry Styles—everything is just working so smooth for them—then *poof!* One day, all their mojo is just gone. They're back at square one again. The reason for the shift isn't that their actions are suddenly bad, nor has it anything to do with their hair products, it's simply because the world has changed around them, as it will around you. (And it will, even for Harry Styles.)

We exist in a complex world. Things change constantly in ways that you have no control over. A new VP replaced the old one and suddenly, your team of researchers is on the chopping block. A dip in the stock market pushes your dream home a few years further down the line. Things change. You react.

This is why it's critical to understand that one group of

actions isn't enough to handle every situation. As the world around you changes, your plans need to adapt. But you don't do this ad hoc. That would go against everything we've taught here. Instead, you need to build an adaptive strategy.

Adaptive strategies can be thought of as a collection of micro-frameworks geared toward solving a multitude of problems. Housed within them is a tight feedback cycle that enables us to figure out if we need to change course as we take action toward our goals. While that might sound complicated, it's actually something we do frequently without labeling each step or even realizing that's what we're doing.

Take fishing competitions, for example. Folks will jump on a boat, scour a lake for several hours, and then someone comes back with the biggest fish. Believe it or not, that is a very complex system. You've got a lot to take into account, least of all the behavior of the fish.

So how does someone win a fishing contest? Well, step one is that they have to *know the fish*. Most competitors have done the research and know what kind of fish live in the lake, where their hangout preferences are, and a general idea of what type of food or bait they like to eat. They want to best understand the environment they will be competing in, so they can overcome any challenges that will occur.

Two, there's a whole process of choosing the right rod, the

tastiest bait, knowing how to reel in a fish, etc. Competitors clearly deploy a multitude of strategies to accomplish the goal. Basically, it's the art of predicting the future so they are prepared for it.

Step three, then, is getting onto the lake, and finding the spots where those fish would hang out. At dawn, they may prefer a warmer-water area after the cool of the night. At dusk, the opposite. But there's no guarantee. You'll see these competitors use their intuition to run to a spot, fish for a few hours, and then decide if it's worth staying or leaving to go to a new spot.

Now, imagine if, instead, the competitor could just see directly under the water. The entire process of searching the lake for the fish would be moot. They would literally just follow the school around, throwing lines right in front of their faces. There's no prediction there, just reaction. However, that's not how fishing works and also not how life works. To fish, they need to do some discovery, make some estimates, and then decide to move on. That's the crux: if you want to be impactful, you have to develop a knack for thinking deeply about the future and hone your skills in predicting what will happen and how you'll adapt to unforeseen changes.

As you can see, adaptive strategies give us great freedom and direction at the same time as we take actions to achieve a goal. The trick is that actions are asymmetric in execution. That is, the level of impact and the amount of ejecta or side effects they can cause may not be equal. So understanding the potential consequences of your actions will help create boundaries for determining whether your actions are impactful.

For example, say your goal is to be famous, so you create a video of you doing something you'd never do in front of your grandmother and it goes viral. Sure you might achieve your goal. You might also lose your job and be ostracized from Thanksgiving dinners. In other words, having an adaptive strategy that subsequently led you to create a video Grandma is proud of might have been a better way to go.

By using them, you will make impactful actions while you adapt, adjust, and keep the end goal in sight, all while things stir around you. Side benefits of adaptive strategies are the reduction in ego, sunk cost, and loss aversion; if you suddenly realize things aren't working toward your goal, you will know the most impactful thing you can do is cut line and move on.

COMPLEX VS COMPLICATED SYSTEMS

I can calculate the movement of stars, but not the madness of men.

—SIR ISAAC NEWTON

A complicated system is like the design for an airplane. Once you know how to build a plane, someone else can use your design and build another. The factors impacting the success of a complicated system, at least in this example, are knowable.

A complex system is what's going on inside an air-traffic control tower. The controllers are constantly adjusting their directions as situations unfold. There is always uncertainty about the next set of conditions. They are forced to deal with random variations (e.g., the weather) and outliers (e.g., a plane hitting a goose).

Adaptive strategies are built to handle complex systems. They help us adapt to situations that are not foreseen in advance. They must account for randomness. In addition to adjusting to constant change and unexpected events, quarterbacks and air-traffic controllers must also deal with emergencies and events that are not within safe odds. The state of being in constant flux with ever-changing parts and people requires perpetual adaptation. So even though the quarterback has a plan of action on how to get the ball down the field and even though he has studied the opposing team's habit's and patterns to know what to expect from them, there is always uncertainty—that sudden downpour that turns the field into a mudslide—about the next set of conditions. Similarly, air-traffic controllers who ultimately have a strategy for bringing in planes safely, are constantly adjusting their directions as situations unfold.

Complicated systems, meanwhile, make us think in a box: once the system is figured out, we work in a particular way with a particular pattern within that system. The nature of that closed system provides a challenge with most problem-solving techniques. By definition, we're applying our existing patterns to new problems. We must be careful to identify when we've moved out of the realm of the complicated and into the space of the complex: when we approach complex systems with tools and algorithms designed for complicated systems, things can go horribly wrong.

Complicated systems, by definition, create an expected environment by reducing variables and uncertainty. Complex systems, on the other hand, are defined by that uncertainty.

We will always exist in a complex system simply because there are people in the system with us. By nature, humans, are in a perpetual state of change. So when humans are involved, you know it's now a complex system; hence the quote from Isaac Newton that we started this chapter with.

When it comes to making an impact, we have to remember that all our actions occur in a complex system. The people, the scenarios, the effort, the effects—it's all quite complex. You might have a set of actions that work beautifully on a complicated problem, but when your manager suddenly changes and all your impact evaluations get thrown out the door, those actions may have to go with them. So the best way to deal with a complex system is to develop adaptive strategies.

THE PREDICTION SWEET SPOT

Adaptive strategies both require and enable you to predict the future because they're based on research and learning about the environment of your complex system. Adaptive strategies guide your decision-making in an uncertain and ever-changing world. With time and practice, you'll learn to find the sweet spot between not waiting long enough and waiting too long to make a decision.

If you're the kind of person who regards decision-making as a reactive activity, then you have probably had little experience predicting the future and may feel uncomfortable just thinking about. Being reactive is easy to do. We wait for the universe to reveal the need to do something or press a decision onto us, and then we react. Given the last-minute constraints put on us at that point, we usually have few options to choose from and we may not be thrilled by any of them. For example, if you have plans to spring the question on your true love on Valentine's Day but wait until February 13 to make reservations for a swanky restaurant to do it in, you might end up having to pop the question by the soft pretzel heater inside your local Target superstore. Granted the pictures you post on Instagram will be funny and cute, but the food and atmosphere may have been more enjoyable for you both if you'd snagged a table at that gastropub you both love.

As you become a student of impact, you'll start to realize that you need to push your decision-making back a bit. The further you are from a "terminal decision," the more options you'll have and the better chance you'll make decisions that create greater impact for you. Thus, a starting point for your playbook of adaptive strategies is to research and learn enough about the system you're in to see where it's going, so you can begin making decisions while you have the most options available, not the least.

But we have to be careful not to project too far into the future. There's a point of diminishing return where the unknowns start to pile up, given that time will adapt and adjust things in ways we couldn't see. As such, our predictions and strategy are mostly useless, since the future is so foggy. Despite this, many people make decisions far out anyway. This is a commonality in real estate. People will buy a home near a piece of land that a big company has purchased to build a new facility. They buy the house because they expect that, in five to eight years, the home will double in value due to proximity to the corporation. While there is some historical evidence in this play, what's occurring is that they are taking on a lot of risk in order to hopefully gain a large reward before others around them get wise to it.

Risk is the keyword to have in mind as you make predictive decisions. The closer you are to a terminal decision, the fewer options you have for impact and you're stuck with making the "best worst decision." More variables, and their potential risk, reveal themselves with an elongated timeline, hence you can create adaptive strategies for problems that you may have to deal with later—or that never materialize, if you plan too far in advance.

As you grow your skills as a student of impact, you'll slowly start to find the sweet spot between those extremes of waiting until the last minute and being forced to make a decision and planning from a too-distant vantage point. You will become an oracle, of sorts, with the ability to define and deploy an adaptive strategy that can weather any changes that might come your way.

And that is the beauty and perfect sense of it all: Your playbook of adaptive strategies for impactful actions will be based on your ability to predict the future. Focusing on the future and the larger picture should consume much of our thinking. Based on this vision, we can set practical goals and guide ourselves and our groups toward them, which is why we need to become masters of the visionary process through practice and experience.

Attaining such mastery will give us tremendous confidence in ourselves, as opposed to the fake confidence of those who are merely grandiose. And when we exude this confidence, people will be drawn to us and want to follow our lead.

With this understanding of complex systems and how adaptive strategies can guide us through them toward impactful actions, it's time to learn how to build our strategies. The next two chapters show you how to first build your Impactful Actions Playbook and then how to execute on the strategy.

CHAPTER 8

SOURCE POTENTIAL ACTIONS

A man finds a lamp, rubs it, and a genie appears.

Excited, the man begins to do what he thinks is expected of him. "I wish for more—" he starts, but the genie holds up his hand like a police officer and stops him.

"You can't wish for more wishes," the genie says.

The man sits and thinks for a moment.

"Okay, then," he finally says. "I wish for more genies."

While a bit tongue in cheek, the above story highlights an important concept: No matter your goal, there's more than one way to accomplish it. We think it's a nicer and less gory version of the adage "there's more than one way to skin a cat."

As you journey on your way to make impact on your goal, you'll inevitably run into barriers, setbacks, politics, red tape, resource restrictions, etc. As such, a single action won't allow you to achieve impact, but rather, you need a set of actions that you can accomplish either linearly or as alternatives as things change.

The point of an Impactful Actions Playbook is to evaluate and list your potential actions that you can use later—potential actions that are based on adaptive strategies. The meta goal is to evaluate all the types of things you can do that would contribute to a positive impact toward your end goal and annotate the information so that you can figure out which one to use and at what time.

To return to our football example, on the sidelines, the play-callers are constantly looking at the field, making decisions, evaluating the context against the options of things they could do, and then passing that information along to the coaches and players. Then both teams settle on the line of scrimmage, get locked into their formations, and wait for a few seconds.

The defense doesn't know for sure what's coming and the offense doesn't know for sure what will happen. Then, when the ball snaps, it looks like chaos breaks out. But if you're a spectator who's familiar with the teams, you'll see plays that look familiar, as if you'd watched these teams rehearse this game hundreds of times. The ideal run through a gap, the perfect pass, the just-in-time tackle, all of them have been done numerous times but with different results. That's because what looks like chaos on the field is really an adaptive strategy at play. On the offensive side, as the quarterback steps back, he already has a set of goals, options, and fallbacks that he's practiced with his team time and time again. When the defense changes, the same play can work but with the leveraging of different options.

As with a quarterback on the field, we must come to terms with the fact that our goal is part of a complex system and thus rife with uncertainty. Since we cannot create plans for every contingency (nor can we create effective plans at the last minute), we make plans that include a readiness to adapt as the future unfolds.

In the business world, as well as sports, we talk about strategy and tactics. Tactics are how to handle smaller situations in various ways. We have to assume a complex system is built of layers of smaller systems, all of which are interwoven. So you can't have one solution to it all but, rather, an estimated set of situations that you can create plans for. As they come up, like a quarterback, you can apply, adapt, iterate, and improve your tactics and your plans.

You create your network of tactics by growing neurons in your brain. Seriously. If you're going to create an Impactful Actions Playbook filled with adaptive strategies that are properly sourced, the brain you have just isn't enough. You need to grow your brain.

You'll do that by researching and absorbing material, finding a template, testing ideas, and teaching others.

After that, you'll get an even bigger brain by reaching out to other people to learn from them. How did they get where they are? What went wrong? What kind of feedback can they give you about your goals? Do they know of any other resources or people who could be useful to you as you build your playbook.

Then you'll label the actions you've gathered to review, modify, and rank each one for its potential for impact. What's the estimated impact? What's the estimated energy? What's the estimated ejecta?

At the end of all of that, you'll have a playbook of potential impactful actions. Ready to get started?

STEP 1: GROW YOUR BRAIN

Science tells us that our brains are composed of millions of neurons that are all interconnected. As electricity flows between them, it lights up the connections it passes while on its way to wherever it's going. Some folks in the field of neuroscience believe this is where creativity comes from, so perhaps it's rather fitting that the lightbulb is a symbol for an idea.

That lighting up happens when you're in the shower and BAM! an idea comes to you. Or when you finally get the solution to something that you've been struggling with, and it comes to you when you're not even thinking about it. Those off times of genius happen because the side pathways lighting up in new signals are making connections in new ways. The more connections, the more neurons, the more chances you'll get creativity, faster.

So to get your brain aggressively growing neurons to come up with ideas for potential actions for your goal, fill it with more opportunities to make connections about that subject. In a word: research.

RESEARCH AND ABSORB MATERIAL

Commonly, what separates novice from expert members of a group is the "blank page problem." Novices, who don't understand the full space of potential actions can often get stalled staring at a blank page, not knowing how or where to start. Experts, however, have seen it all so many times that starting is mundane to them.

Your goal then, as a novice, is to grow your brain as quickly as possible.

To start, you must become an obsessive researcher of things around your goal. To help you do that, we have a process. We call it the Colt's Patented-Not Patented technique for becoming brilliant at something really quickly. It works like this:

1. Copy and paste as much research into a single document as possible. It's fine if it's hundreds of pages; the goal is to accumulate information, context, and fine-grain details into a single place, so your brain can see it all at once. Most of your research is going to come from various sources and this step helps you homogenize the data. Keep it in one location for evaluation. Side note: you'll know you're done researching once you stop finding novel information and rabbit holes to go down.

2. Create patterns and buckets. Once you've got a critical mass of research, you'll begin to see subtle themes, trends, and patterns emerge. And each new piece of information you add will seem to fit into these large narratives or buckets. Let's say you find a new website with great new details on your tasks. After your document gets big enough, you can paste that data into a location that's relative to other information you've found. After a while, this starts to create a mock table of contents, where big ideas start to emerge in this space.

3. Break apart and drill in. Once your document gets big enough and you can see buckets emerge, you can now separate the ideas into smaller documents. Copy and paste the big ideas into new docs and you can then drill down for each one of them, easily being able to refine your queries and research as you go along.

If done right, you can spend maybe fourteen hours on Step 1, four hours on Step 2, and two hours on Step 3. So within twenty hours of work, you might have amassed an amazing amount of detail about a subject area you've never known about before.

The next step is to take that information and create a pattern you can emulate, or you can create a template and emulate one of the successful people you just learned from.

FIND A TEMPLATE

A famous game company had built one of the most successful MMO (massive multiplayer) games of all time. It completely overtook the previous genre-defining game that had been in the top spot for over a decade. While many called this luck, it was anything but. Four years prior, productivity at the company started to drop. It turns out that all the engineers and artists were spending their lunch hours playing this amazing MMO and lunch was starting to take all afternoon. Through their obsessive playing, they realized something: Many people were having fun but didn't like some of the core mechanics of the game. They spotted a few areas that could improve and wanted to see how much more fun the game could be with those things changed.

So a small group of people set off to rebuild the game from scratch to get a version they could play with and tweak. Once they did that, they began making small changes to the game to improve it to the way they wanted it. They continued this process over and over again until the game looked, felt, and played completely differently. Two years later, they launched their version with a new name, which changed the gaming industry forever. Their success started by literally duplicating the mechanics of a previous video game and then they made subtle changes, just slightly improving upon it each time, until it reached a level of fun they enjoyed.

That is an amazing way to get to a goal. If you think about every project, game, or idea you look at, you'll see it was a derivation of something that came before it, only with slight tweaks, modifications, or changes in idea.

And if you can't create a template, you have another option: steal like an artist.

Good artists copy, great artists steal.

—PABLO PICASSO

While it's a very famous line, did Picasso literally steal other painters' work? No. He merely imitated his favorite artists a lot. But what did he mean? And why does it make sense for artists to imitate one another?

Austin Kleon is a writer who draws. He's written multiple *New York Times* bestsellers about the creative process of being an artist. He encourages you to not worry about being original and just focus on getting started. Kleon's advice is worth following.

When you're starting out, it'll be hard to come up with ideas about how to do things. But you can always start with rebuilding what someone else has done. From that point, you'll eventually start to deviate from their work and start making things your own, bit by bit. As you do this repeatedly, you'll eventually discover that there are areas you can't duplicate: techniques you don't know, technology you don't understand, or skills you don't have. That is where you start to insert your skills, processes, or technologies and that's when things start to become your own.

If you're familiar with the movie *Finding Forrester,* you'll see a beautiful representation of this idea. In the movie, an American writer played by Sean Connery gives a paragraph from an early writing of his and asks a young Rob Brown to start with his words, but "make it his own story."

This type of idea is one of the most powerful tools at your disposal. So why don't some people do it? Many consider it an ethically grey area: By starting with someone else's plan, content, or lifestyle, they feel that it's a level of theft that doesn't sit well with their core values. Others are fine with starting using someone else's work but feel they don't have the skills to make it their own. And still others think there are just too many places to start.

When confronted with what seems like unlimited options, how do you pick templates to use or people to emulate? The trick is to look for clues in the environmental data that leads to the early success but isn't the reason for continued success. For example, if you want to become a famous wrestler, following the life of Dwyane "The Rock" Johnson might be a really good choice. Sadly though, you might lack some of the distinct advantages he had—including that his dad was a famous wrestler as well—he may not be the best choice for you.

If you'd like to become a famous singer, there are thousands of stories you can copy. But if you're a white girl from Oklahoma, you might not be able to follow the same path as Jay-Z. Instead maybe mimicking the world of Taylor Swift would be more beneficial.

The point is some templates are closer to who you are today and some templates are closer to your goal. You have to find a template that fits your ethical bias and technical skill-set code, while also showing a clear path toward your goal.

But there's more than one way to skin a cat (sorry, we just had to use it or risk repeating the genie story). So yes, when applied to your true goal, if you want to be a famous singer, find a person who has done that, who comes from a background similar to yours. Want to be a millionaire? Find someone who did it first and set up your investments in a similar way. But in all instances you'll need to make changes based on your context and risk factors.

Interestingly enough, we see the concept of stealing like an artist is hard-wired into life on planet Earth. There is not a more specific example than human existence itself. When we start out, we are taught how to view the world, take on tasks, and be a human in the same way our parents or caregivers do. They teach us their ways, their processes, and help us avoid mistakes that they had made. This builds a framework for who we are and how we behave. But soon (usually around those teenage years) our chemistry changes and we start to push away from what we've learned. We want to do it our own way, find our own path. By the time we're in our 20s or 30s, this process has continued and we've taken what was once a solid foundation but completely made it our own.

Like it or not, this process is hard-wired into who we are as a species and as a society—embrace it. Leverage the work your predecessors did, then create a template and make it your own.

Once you grow your brain by growing neurons, you should be in a place where you feel lit up, inspired, and excited about all the avenues you have available to you to take impactful action toward your goal. The next step, though, before you head into execution, is to grow that big brain you have. That can be handy if you don't think you have the time to grow your brain or you grew it as far as you think is possible but you're not sure if it's enough. In both cases, you need to get a bigger brain.

STEP 2: GET A BIGGER BRAIN

After doing Step 1, we often realize there's a limit to how fast we can grow our neurons and how quickly we can gain experience in an area. And that can be a problem.

It can take a long time to go from novice to master. So if you can't spend twenty-four hours a day researching, you need other options. And let's face it, if you're reading this book, chances are you have a deadline for reaching your goal. Perhaps it's even a performance evaluation in six months. In that case, you may realize that there's a time limit on a project, which puts a limit on your research time and neuron-growing time.

So even if the only way to really become a master is to lock yourself in a closet and research and test and analyze for the next decade, that's not always plausible. And it's seldom fun.

You have to find the difference between what is ideal versus what's doable. And that's when you do the amount of research you can, given the time that you have. You're still pushing the edges of your knowledge and growing your brain. To make up for the time you can't spend researching, you get other brains involved.

Ed Catmull wrote a fantastic book called *Creativity, Inc.* wherein he details the workings of Pixar, the company renowned for creating some of the most iconographic stories and movies in the 90s and 2000s.

Pixar revolutionized a unique process of daily creative review where every part of a movie created on one day was cut to shreds the next morning by the rest of the team. On a project that might last three years, that equates to hundreds of thousands of scenes that have been done, received feedback, and redone. The results speak for themselves.

What the Pixar team tapped into here was a realization that one brain isn't enough. By including other brains, they—and you—effectively increase the current set of neurons working on a goal and leverage that creativity for new ideas.

The end result: you've got a bigger brain to think of the problem for you.

Much like you can copy someone's template, you can learn from others' experience. In the past, we were only able to communicate with and tap into the experiences of people within our geographically accessible community. If you want to know whether the berries on a particular bush are harmful, you might observe someone eating them first. If they skipped off happy and satisfied, you would eat them too. If they keeled over unconscious, you'd probably make other plans. Today, our accessible community is limited only by our imagination of how to reach out to them.

When we engage with others as we think about and plan for our future, they may know of or detect potential problems and pitfalls outside our scope of awareness. They help give us a map to the minefield we are walking through. And they prove to us that we can be optimistic about getting where we want to be.

Catching errors before they become a crisis can save money, time, and reputation. The more errors we catch early, the fewer problems there are to solve when the cost in money, time, or reputation can be prohibitive.

As you grow your brain, one of the key questions to ask is: how did you get here?

ASK THEM HOW THEY GOT THERE

As mentioned earlier, you probably aren't the first person to do whatever it is you want to do. There are others. Get them in a room—either real or virtual, but make sure they are there of their own free will—and ask them how they achieved the thing you want to achieve. It's that simple.

Given that you are asking people about their success, most people will be over the moon to talk to you about their story. Indulge their ego. Ask for fine details about what made the difference in success and failure for them. And take the time to annotate their story with contextual changes, meaning: what's different from when they did it and now? Did they start with more money or experience than you have today? Were there corporate differences that enabled their actions to be valid? Have the tax laws changed since then?

Basically, everyone's success story is built, in some way, on the analysis and exploitation of the system they're involved with, combined with a bit of solid luck. For some reason, we downplay luck in success. We like to think of luck as the point where preparation meets opportunity. But don't discount the role that luck plays in the success of people you're interviewing.

It's important to ask this question to as many people as possible. If you do it properly, you'll start to see a pattern emerge. You'll be able to identify common environmental or societal influences and common actions that each one took that allowed them to get to where they are, which thankfully, is exactly where you want to go. You can use the knowledge to start plotting a (metaphorical) map of all the different paths people have taken in order to achieve the success that you're seeking.

It's worth noting, however, that memory is a lousy medium. It's very easily manipulated, has a poor shelf life, and tends to get more positive or negative with time. As such, when you discuss their paths to success, it's important to not stay at the surface. You need to ask for more details about what their path looked like, which brings us to our second step: ask them what went wrong.

ASK THEM WHAT WENT WRONG AND FOR FEEDBACK

There's a classic old-timey saying that goes something like "consequences teach better than lectures." Ironically, people frequently said it when lecturing teens but regardless, there's some proof in those words. As many times as someone tries to warn us not to touch the hot stove when we're young, some people just won't trust advice. They have to burn their fingers before they realize the truth of the situation.

A key characteristic of students of impact, however, is that they listen to the lectures of what went wrong, so they can avoid the consequences of discovering it for themselves. There's nothing like learning from someone else's mistakes.

Mistakes aside, people who were where you are now probably know more about what you are trying to do. So ask them for advice. Get feedback on how they would solve the problem you have now. How would they proceed toward your goal? What do they think of your plans?

Remember your goal is to use the increased neurons from your research along with the "bigger brain" of the people who are where you want to be to source actions you can take to impact your goals. Asking them is the optimal way to source new ideas. All you have to do is ask a few questions and let them do all the work of solving the problem for you.

There's an added benefit here, which is grounds for a whole separate section that we'll discuss later: If this person happens to be someone you could collaborate with to achieve your goals, then asking them to get involved early makes them a stakeholder in your plan. They now have skin in the game. No one wants to give bad advice that fails, especially if they will be affected by the failure. Once they've given you advice about how they'd solve the situation, they will have some ego and inclination to see that through. And if by chance it does fail, you'll quickly see them step up to offer alternative advice as well.

Probably the most important data to glean from growing your brain and asking others for advice is surfacing any unknown problems that your actions might be producing. The goal is to reduce uncertainty and these folks have a vision in to your future that enables them to do just that.

After you've asked questions and received answers, take the time to filter their feedback. You won't be able to activate all of their suggestions due to various circumstances—it could be new tax laws were enacted and you can no longer take refuge in Bermuda or maybe a resource is simply no longer available. Regardless, you may have higher risks or you have context that would make the actions unachievable.

Then before you bid adieu, see if there is anything else you can learn.

ASK THEM ABOUT UNKNOWN RESOURCES

Folks who have already achieved your goal have a vast set of "wish I would have known that earlier" comments. Most of them involve leveraging techniques or resources they didn't know about before. Discover what they are.

GET SOME CONTEXT: STORYTIME WITH COLT

I had a breakthrough in my career around 2012. I had the desire to produce a new project that would help developers understand how to build games in a web browser (a cliché by today's terms) and I was sure it would help the company's bottom line. My problem was that it would take me months and months to do it. But when talking to a few other engineers about it, they suggested I take a look at who had any operational budget and ask if they'd lend it to a vendor to build it for me.

My mind was blown. That was a thing I could do? I could take $200,000 and turn it into a fully working game in six months while I was still plugging away at my day job? Wowsa! And the best part: I got credit for both! That broke my brain and has since driven a huge amount of my planning and behavior. I now always ask myself "Is there someone else who can benefit from doing this instead?" Basically, I'm calling back to the fact that I *could* do it, but if someone else can gain credit too, then it's even better.

There are numerous avenues to find resources that others have used to get to a goal similar to what you're reaching for. Here are some of those avenues.

EXPLOITING ALTERNATIVES

Alternative solutions to a problem are a gift gained only through struggling your way through. Consistently, the most impactful members of an organization are the ones who have "seen this before" and can avoid problems and take advantage of opportunities or steer their projects into alternative methods without sinking the ship. Those who lack impact, conversely, don't seem to have enough perspective on the company's overall operations to present an alternative view and constantly get stuck when problems arise. By asking what alternatives they would suggest to reach the same goal, you're asking them to come up with a variety of innovative approaches to a given situation, given their expertise (which you obviously don't have).

Identifying Allies

Allies are effective in most contexts but when it comes to achieving your goals in a professional setting, they are paramount. The right allies can propel you forward, while the wrong ones can drag you down. Sometimes we like to think we know whom the best people to work with are, but during your questioning, you might be amazed to find new allies you didn't know about before. This leverages the networking effect and can save you oodles of time.

ASK THEM WHOM ELSE YOU CAN ASK

The final step of your process should be to ask for an introduction to someone else who is closer to your goal. Find that person and ask the same questions.

When you start the process of growing your bigger brain,

you'll most likely start with people in your close proximity: friends, coworkers, people at parties, the cashier at your local grocer. If you stop there, you'll never tap into the vast amount of knowledge and experience of people you *haven't met yet.*

That's actually critically important—being able to ask someone, "Can you introduce me to someone else who has successfully done this before who could tell me their story?" allows you to also build a bigger network of stakeholders and people who are interested in your success. If you're lucky, you might even source a mentor or someone who becomes invested in your success, rather than just being interested.

ACTIONS THAT MAKE OTHER THINGS EASIER

Humans are bad at things, so we often need to modify the world around us to keep ourselves from fudging things up. For example, if you'd like to lose weight, an action to take might be to remove all the high-calorie snacks from your house. While these actions might not show up in your research or in your interviews, you might need to source actions that help put guardrails on yourself. This is a nice question to ask people while you're surveying them: Ask them what types of steps you could take to better reduce catastrophe. Depending on how creative they are, you might get some wild answers!

After you get a bigger brain and then grow your brain, the next step is to take everything you've learned and give it a name.

STEP 3: LABELING FOR IMPACT

Now that you have a plethora of amazing actions that you've just gathered from potentially hundreds of sources, it's important to put them into your processing framework. Each one will be personalized to the presenter and may or may not make sense in your current context. As such, as you ingest this data, it's critical to modify and rank each potential action in terms of impact.

Remember, we want to identify only a few core things:

- What is the estimated impact this action will have on my end goal?
- What is the amount of energy it will take to achieve this impact?
- What will be the ejecta of this impact?

WHAT'S THE ESTIMATED IMPACT?

This is one of the first questions you should ask about an action. It's important to identify this early since it helps you very quickly quantize or remove bad ideas before you even start the more costly efforts of evaluating energy and ejecta.

To do this, you need to clearly understand, or at least estimate to the best of your abilities, whether you can quickly sense that this is negative effort. In which case, you can drop the action immediately. If you can't see a net positive impact, then put it on the back burner. And things that seem like a positive impact should be put at the top of your list, sorted by the biggest gains.

WHAT'S THE ESTIMATED ENERGY?

Remember, *energy* can mean many things and is usually a subject of the resources involved and that you're looking at it in terms of trade-offs.

Some things will cost more *money* but take less *time*. Other things will cost more *emotional* effort but will reduce *negotiation* effort.

The problem is that now that you've sourced a bunch of actions, each one will be written in a different form of expected energy cost. Your job is to try to unify this into as few separate buckets as possible. And an easy place to start with those labels is with *Time, Money, Emotion.*

WHAT'S THE ESTIMATED EJECTA?

As you start surveying the system, you'll start to notice how some actions can cause other actions in the system. As you label things, it's important to note this ejecta in as full form as possible. You should be very blunt and real about the ejecta since this is the most dangerous place to lie to yourself.

If you wrongly estimate impact, you could waste time. If you wrongly estimate energy, you can waste resources. However, if you wrongly estimate ejecta, then you can create a whole new world of problems that you have to spend time and resources solving. As such, this is the one you want to get right and make sure you properly, and truthfully, document it.

DON'T SORT, JUST DOCUMENT

It's important to note that during this time, your goal is to categorize and label. Sorting will happen as a process of executing the playbook, which we'll talk about in the next chapter.

You are almost ready to execute on everything! Congratulate yourself! You've got actions!

YOU'VE GOT ACTIONS!

The point of this entire process is to quickly and efficiently source the world around you to figure out the actions you can take to achieve your goals. By researching, finding a template, and growing your brain, you've effectively created a process that lets you work backward from the end goal to create projects and actions that are flexible but yet still achieve specific intentions.

As you get better at this, you'll start to spend much less energy sourcing decisions about what actions to take. You'll have stronger neuron connections that will allow you to source creative ideas and solutions faster. You'll do that by evaluative thinking to bring the future to the present in an effort to reduce uncertainty. You'll also do it by thinking in permutation space; by visualizing or walking through the situations with the understanding that you can't see everything, but you can try to eliminate uncertainty where possible.

And now you're ready to execute.

CHAPTER 9

EXECUTING THE SYSTEM

Having a list of actions by themselves isn't really valuable. It's like having a Pinterest page devoted to romantic recipes. That page by itself won't ensure you'll make the perfect dinner to woo that special someone. You need to set a goal for the dinner (lobster macaroni and cheese, for example) and then figure out a plan of actions—that is, create an executional framework that involves researching the ingredients and tools needed, surveying the supplies you have on hand as well as your experience in the kitchen to determine where you need input from others, and creating a timeline. You also need to figure out the right actions to take—the impactful actions—as you work through that executional framework.

Think of your Impactful Actions Playbook in terms of that executional framework. After narrowing the Pinterest page down to a couple of recipes, doing your homework, and then creating a plan of actions, dealing with impetus, and measuring your effectiveness toward the end goal, you have the ultimate meal. You also created an Impactful Actions Playbook to achieve that goal.

But while it all sounds simple, it can be hard to figure out just...

WHERE DO I START?

In any approach toward a goal, you need to identify which actions are going to be the most valuable first steps. Thankfully, you've now got a list of actions you could take along with some ranking data that helps you understand the impact, effort, and ejecta of those actions. If you've taken the time, your list of actions will also include opportunities to improve your emotional foundation and do what other prep work that needs to be done before you can start your journey toward your goal in earnest.

A good place to start is to do an audit of your low-level goals and address any deficiencies. That will eliminate any skewed thinking about what you should be doing. Then, move on up the hierarchy of needs and address your socio-emotional foundation. Again, you're trying to avoid issues down the line. Once both these areas are covered, you can finally start looking at the true steps toward your goal.

At this point, the first actions to take should reflect those that find a balance among low effort, high impact, and low ejecta. These will allow you to test the waters, make some earnest progress, and get feedback on things.

ITERATION AND EXECUTION

Everybody has a plan until they get punched in the mouth.

—MIKE TYSON

We have to remember that taking actions toward your goal is a bit of an iterative process. You'll need to try some things, see if your estimates of effort, impact, and ejecta were right, and then update your rankings, lists, and your plans accordingly. This is all part of the adaptive strategies we discussed before. You adapt after trying some things and getting feedback.

To get that feedback as you take your actions, you'll need to evaluate their success against some heuristics that fall into two categories:

1. When you've completed an action/task
2. While you're still executing an action/task

Because we understand that the environment we're operating in is complex, we understand that these items can change regularly and, thus, we need to re-evaluate things constantly. To get a better understanding of what's involved in this, let's dig into evaluations in a bit more detail.

UPON COMPLETION OF AN ACTION

The point of having lots of potential actions is that they are small enough to accomplish, yet large enough to actually do some work. As such, you'll eventually be checking off actions from your list while seeing slow and steady progress toward your goal. When an action is completed, either for better or worse, you will need to run a brief postmortem on how it went. Each time you check off an action, ask yourself:

Did I succeed at this action?

As we've discussed, you shouldn't take an action without some sense of what the outcome should be. Therefore, it will be clear whether you've hit the target outcome or not.

If you hit it, ask: *did the impact, effort, and ejecta match my expectations?*

This is an important question. Early on in your path to being a student of impact, you'll be bad at estimating these things and so each time you get a chance, you need to re-evaluate how you're doing in terms of those estimates.

If you did not hit it, ask: *what information should I use to re-evaluate my rankings of actions I've already got?*

If you got things wrong, then it's worth taking a quick look through everything else to see what you need to update. If your assumptions are off in one area, then it might be off in multiple places.

Did I fail at this action?

Understand that failure is a natural part of the learning process and that not all failures create the same effects or have the same repercussions. So you may need to ask, "What does failure mean for this action? And, who gets to define it?" That's a whole other book in itself, but since you're already reading this one, here's a short-and-sweet discussion.

Failure often doesn't mean what you think it does. Sometimes we put too much gravitas on the consequences of failure when, in reality, it's not as bad as we had anticipated. (And to be fair, sometimes we get it wrong in the other direction as well.) As far as your career goes, though, the use of the word failure really only makes sense if it's related to something you did that created a negative impact for you (thus moving your goals backward). This concept of failure translates rather well to the majority of your career situations: if you fail at a big presentation, chances are that your performance will not sit well with your manager, who will then become less likely to promote you as fast as the time you've set yourself to hit your goals.

So perhaps the right way to look at failure to determine what it means is to look at what the outputs of that failure are; to consider how stakeholders, relationships, laws, or observers might react in a negative way; and estimate how that might impact your overall goals. For example, you might not have landed that big meeting but maybe that really wasn't the point. Maybe the point was just to show that your team could up the number of customer meetings you had this year, regardless of the quality of those meetings. As such, bombing the presentation, then, really wasn't a failure.

Going through the process of evaluating your potential failures helps solidify you against the system you're operating in and steadies you for your own mental sanity. That is, if you have a general sense of what failure means and have come to the conclusion that it ain't that bad, then you've taken a load off your shoulders.

Once you've made yourself stable regarding failure, it's time to look with a keen eye at what caused the failure in the first place. First, since failure is the same as negative impact, you have to figure out what caused negative impact to happen. Was it that your impact was too low, thus hurting expectations of others? Was your ejecta too high, thus hurting relationships? Or possibly most important, was there some problem with your foundations or planning that caused a failure you weren't expecting?

Getting this type of feedback is critical, as it factors into your plans for further actions and it can help you gain perspective so that you can address the issues before failures happen again.

Once you're clear on whether your action was a success or failure and why, you may know what your next action step should be. But if you don't, then you'll need to go back and review the potential steps you can take. Again, you will want to pick actions that are balanced among low effort, high impact, and low ejecta. In many cases, you'll have to re-prioritize or sort them, because one action may hinge on the work of a prior action.

WHILE EXECUTING ACTIONS

Once we start executing our system, we have to be aware that things can and will change. You can't just design a plan and let it run. Your system needs flexibility that allows you to course correct when things don't go your way. The world will change around you. Because of that, as you execute, you'll find you need to change your rankings and estimates on impact, effort, and ejecta. And as new data comes in you may need to figure out which (if any) of the actions on your list might require updating.

When Things Go South

Sometimes failure doesn't happen at the end of a process and, instead, the signs appear while you're in action. That's when it's time to cut bait and run. There can be numerous factors at play here. Sometimes it just doesn't work and, at other times, the parameters grow beyond your control. Regardless of why, when those things happen, the best thing to do is drop the action and move on to something else.

Failure can produce such fear in us that we push through on doomed actions despite the growing evidence in front of us. Oftentimes, we're more worried about being criticized for our failures than the failures themselves and that points more to a social dynamic than it does an absolute dynamic. Again, you need to keep focused on your end goal, not the millions of actions that make it up or what other people are thinking of us. Those are disposable.

A benefit of the research we do in this system is that it helps you source how things *can* go wrong. By doing so, you become less afraid because the research helps you prepare for potential failure as best you can. Then, if something does go wrong, you can handle it and know how to act. More importantly, you'll know it's okay to fail and that failure is part of the process sometimes.

When Things Get Interrupted

Even when failing is not evident, things can go awry in such a way that you discover certain actions may need to bubble up or down in priority due to other factors. For example, things can suddenly become URGENT when they used to just be IMPORTANT, and thus, should bubble up to the top of your list, otherwise the ejecta could be bad.

- **Urgent:** Things that have negative consequences in the immediate twenty-four-hour timeframe. Keep in mind this extends to others as well; answering an email that unblocks a development team of twenty is urgent since the production lost is a huge risk.
- **Important:** Things that will have negative consequences in the medium timeframe of weeks.

The need to shift in priorities to deal with an URGENT or IMPORTANT impetus might be a short-term interruption or it could result in a worldview change that cascades to other actions. (For example, if you get your promotion, you might suddenly get rid of all the actions related to this promotion.)

Because being blindsided by the need to prioritize can be a bit disorienting, we suggest regularly re-evaluating your actions against your core goal and adjusting and adapting them as needed. That requires measuring your impact on the goal to date and comparing that to the energy put in and expected yet. You'll also need to re-evaluate the potential ejecta and ask if the action is still worth the effort. By doing this, you can ensure your priorities are where they need to be.

When Things Join Forces, or Not

A third reason you may change course with your actions is when you see how some actions can be grouped together or perhaps split apart. Sometimes details come into play in such a way that you are provided visibility into your tasks and spaces. When that happens, it's possible that you discover two steps you thought were distinct are really one. To return to the lobster mac and cheese dinner goal, perhaps you originally had such separate action steps as 1) picking out a live lobster from a fishmonger and 2) heading over to that place that makes handmade pasta for the macaroni. But after checking your bank account, you realize it would be economically beneficial to merge those two steps and purchase a premade frozen version of the dinner and call it a day.

Rinse, Recycle, Repeat

As we've mentioned before, adaptive strategies are all about getting feedback, making adjustments, and keeping an eye on your goals. You're expected to continue to grow your brain, use bigger brains, evaluate your goals, test yourself, and check that you're doing the right things. It's a full process that focuses on clear movement toward a goal.

Just remember, success isn't a magic formula. Sure, occasionally someone wins the lottery and someone else inherits a fortune large enough to purchase Guatemala. But no one becomes an NBA star the first time they pick up a basketball. No one performs at Carnegie Hall the first time they place rosin on their violin. And for the overwhelmingly vast majority of us, achieving success at work and building wealth requires skills and expertise that we can gain only after a series of steps and an amount of time passes, so that we can evaluate our steps to know how far, how close, or whether we are successful. And knowing is half the battle.

SETTING PRIORITIES

You may have noticed whether you're re-evaluating your actions after they've been completed or while they're still in process, that we've mentioned the need to prioritize or reprioritize. Whether we're blindsided by an URGENT change requiring us to reprioritize or we've successfully completed a task and are wondering what to do next, or are somewhere in between, we like to use a trick we borrowed from real estate entrepreneur Gary Keller. In his book, *The One Thing*, he encourages readers to approach each day by thinking about the one thing that will have the most impact on them achieving a goal.

We like to use that "One Thing" concept as a way to prioritize actions. To bring it back to that romantic dinner, what's the one thing you need to do, to focus on, when you first begin making a plan? Well, the meal. The goal, right? You need to know exactly what you're going to make. You can't buy ingredients, choose the right wine, or even preheat an oven until you know exactly what you're making.

Next up—What is the one thing that needs to be done after the meal is chosen? Review the recipes to ensure you have the skills and resources to make the various foods.

Next? Here, your one thing will be to evaluate where your skills and resources might need to be enhanced by someone or something.

And on and on it will go. Each one thing will properly set you up for the next one thing.

Notice we're talking about monotasking here, one thing at a time. And each one thing will build on the previous one thing. Your priorities will be ticked off the list in order of most important in this way. And in the case of your romantic dinner, you'll have the candles ordered from Amazon and the perfect playlist at the ready for a successful night or morning, if you're doing a brunch kind of thing.

TEST SOME STUFF FOR CHEAP AND EASY

One final note about execution: if it's possible and you have the time, why not test a few actions to see what works, what doesn't, and accidentally discover new avenues of failure.

Failures are essential because they show you gaps in your process or make you notice all the other steps you haven't considered. Failures will generate a whole new set of actions you never considered before. Welcome failure!

Of course, it's never wise to remortgage your house and dump all your money into an idea or system you haven't tested. You are going to want to try things out, small and quiet, in ways where you can fail without too many negative side effects coming from those failures. You can do this by scaling down various actions in the Playbook so that the impact, risk, and costs are much smaller. For example, you might want to build that new ground-breaking product to create value for your company, just as your mentor did. But you don't have their connections or experience at the company. So you start smaller. Can you get coworkers to give feedback on the idea over lunch, rather than pitching to the VP directly? By doing that, you'll find you can suss out problems quite easily.

A positive side effect of testing for failure is that you can get hands-on learning in your domain space. Up until this point, you've been researching and gathering data. At this stage, you can start getting real feedback to help you, figure out the context you're working in, and remove some of the unknowns before embarking on the whole plan.

PLAN + EXECUTION = IMPACT

Joanna has had enough. She read the book. She absorbed the data. Now she's ready to make change.

She has decided she wants to be an engineering director at a Fortune 500 company. This is a good-enough goal since it's specific (role, title, and scope) but also gives her the wiggle room to achieve it in different scopes (she can be at ANY Fortune 500 company). She asks herself why this goal matters to her and she understands that she has a desire to organize people toward a bigger vision. She likes thinking about big-picture items and, really, the pay isn't bad either. (Hey, a girl's gotta eat, right?)

Joanna then sets out to gather her research for her actions. She starts by booking time with some of the engineering directors at her current company. She asks them about their paths to their position and what their roles entail. She uses their answers to build a list of things she'll need to prepare for. She also gets introduced to directors and VPs at other companies, with whom she builds some recurring mentorship sessions. She makes sure to ask all of them about what resources they might have to leverage and how decisions are made about whom to promote into the role. She quickly learns that the position is just as much about political management as it is about technical management and all the crazy decisions that a big company might make in deciding to promote someone to director...or not.

Soon Joanna has a very clear list of actions that could be available to her to move forward. She realizes at the onset that her political savvy isn't as strong as it needs to be and she doesn't have enough experience leading big projects that interact with VP-level stakeholders. Also she finds that she gets flustered easily and tends to internalize feedback from higher-ups, rather than taking it as feedback for improvement. Not to mention, she'd need quite a number of promotions to get to director level.

She's still intent on her goal, though, so she starts by addressing those issues first. She uses the resources she has (both personal and what her company can offer) to increase her skills in negotiation, strategic planning, and political acumen. She sets her short-term sights on what it takes for the fastest promo she can grab in the system she's working in. She clearly picks projects that matter and provide visibility toward that goal while also aggressively shoring up cracks in her foundational items. As she executes projects, some of them fail and some of them succeed but because Joanna's vision is set far enough in the future, the failures don't dissuade her. She looks at each stumble as a learning moment.

Her first promo lands without a hitch. Those around her quickly point her out as being "in the impact club" and all of her admin chain notes that she's on the fast path to good things. But Joanna is now a realist; she knows that with each promotion, her job changes a little. So she comes back to her actions and throws out things that don't matter anymore and she starts the process of interviewing people to figure out what's next and what her new options are.

Over time, Joanna hits a major stumbling block. Her current company won't promote her because there's no opportunities at that level in the company. But she's crafty and confident. She saw this coming months ago because she'd been interviewing folks at that level and realized that none of them were moving on any time soon. That's why she started looking at opportunities in other companies: to see if there's growth available. In doing so, she's been taking interviews and quickly realizes how rusty her skills are in doing engineering examples on a whiteboard. She sets new short-term goals to improve those skills, knowing that it's the lynchpin to potentially getting hired at the next level.

Her persistence pays off. She's able to land a role at a higher position at a slightly larger company. Effectively, she got the promotion she wanted but had to look outside her previous company to find it. But now she's in a new space and has to start all over again: interviewing folks at the next level, figuring out what it takes to get promoted.

Joanna's vision takes time to execute. Years go by and with each month, her skills grow tremendously. Her focus changes in some places and narrows or expands in others. She repeats the process of planning, taking action, and focusing on impact. When she stumbles, she doesn't let it stop her; she knows that it's part of the process and the next objective is just around the corner. Likewise, Joanna starts to pace herself. She isn't a robot and there's life outside of work. She takes the time to grow her family, takes vacations, and enjoys the world. Her goals haven't changed but she's aware that there's more to life than just her career. With the right focus, she keeps failing and succeeding. It's all part of the journey.

Lo and behold, the day finally comes. Joanna's been executing as a senior engineering lead for a mid-major tech company and they just launched a huge feature that got them buzz in all the proper news publications. That's when an old friend reaches out. One of the directors Joanna interviewed long ago sends her a congratulations email and asks to get some coffee. Over coffee, he pitches Joanna on a new engineering director opening that's about to come up, which he thinks she'd be perfect for.

PLAN, ACT, IMPACT

With Playbook in hand, you're now a member of the impact club. By following the steps here, you bring your goals within reach. You know how to make informed predictions about the future and you have the strategy to adjust your tactics and actions when the inevitable changes that are part of a complex system occur.

Remember, however, as a student of impact, you never stop learning.

CONCLUSION

One of the lead characters in the show *West World* tells a story about when he was a child, and his family adopted a dog. The dog had been a race dog and was bred from puppyhood to chase a stuffed rabbit around the pitch and try as hard as it can to catch it. The dog spent all of its life trying to catch this rabbit and it never did because it's a race dog and that's how dog racing works. The rabbit is not a real rabbit and it's just there to motivate the dog to run.

So they adopt the dog and bring it home and they love the dog. He really enjoys running. And one day the dog gets out off leash and actually chases down a real rabbit. He catches it and kills it. At that point, the character on *West World* says, the dog experienced "human despair and tragedy all at one time." The dog's entire life had been built around catching a rabbit. When he finally caught it, he'd achieved his ultimate goal. Even though he's a simple animal, he had more life in him, yet with no goal left, the dog became depressed.

Don't be like the dog. Don't have only one goal. In fact, the more you become a student of impact (a schooling from which you will never graduate), you will realize that goals go beyond work and beyond hitting a number on a scale. They are not what gives you purpose in life. If you let them do that, you will be like the dog after it caught the rabbit.

Instead, be like Alexander Hamilton.

SET YOUR MIND ON TIME

It's important to realize that you are mortal. Regardless of any personal beliefs about what might happen to your consciousness when you die, pretty much everyone agrees that your time on this earth, in this form, is limited. This means that you have a limited amount of time in order to realize and achieve your goals.

If you're familiar with the Broadway production *Hamilton*, you'll know that frequently in that show, people refer to the amount of work Hamilton does, to the fact that he's never satisfied, and that he's constantly pursuing larger and larger goals.

The character of Death is also predominant in the show. That's because the show's creator, Lin-Manuel Miranda, understood that the real Alexander Hamilton had a close connection to death. He'd lost his parents, his uncle, and many other people who were very close to him. He knew his time was limited and that he needed to make the best of it while he could.

I imagine death so much, it feels like a memory.
—LIN MANUEL MIRANDA, *HAMILTON*.

That sense of a potentially limited mortality is something that must permeate your daily mode as well. Use it to instill a sense of urgency in your life and your actions. After all, the most important resource you have is time.

To be clear, this does not mean you get to live the cliché story of ignoring family and friends for the sake of a career goal. My hope is that during this book, I've instilled a sense of balance in your actions. You must aggressively engage in managing your time and realizing the joy of life as well as the accomplishment of your goals and impact.

Embrace the concept of compound interest: the more value, skills, and successes you can generate early on, the more and greater the results later. Focus on gaining a true goal and then gaining as many skills—as deeply as you can— around that goal.

Set yourself upon the path of execution with aggressive focus. Since you're early in your journey, focus on trial and error to amass knowledge and gain insight into the world around you. Don't be afraid to explore and create a foundation of knowledge that you'll build on over time. This will pay off over time, as the fifty-year-old version of yourself will see much higher prosperity and success in life.

If, when you're further along in life, you use your shorter runway to create hyper-focus in your actions and goals, that focus will allow you to ignore distractions and noise and achieve successes. Likewise, being further along, you may have access to resources, extra time, or social connections that can help you on your way to achieve your goals. Lean on the communities that you've built to achieve the value you're looking for.

Again, time is the most important resource you have. It's something that you lose on a day-to-day basis and you must protect it, guard it, and leverage it to produce impact in your life.

A FINAL NOTE

Once you become a student of impact, your life will start to change. You'll begin to see the world in new ways. You'll start to make significant impact, which will result in significant changes in your life, business, and relationships. You'll start to observe negative behaviors in others that you can identify as unhelpful and you can start to see how those actions hurt their goals and progress in life.

You have cultivated the skills to rise above the moment and not be drawn into their drama. You'll also recognize how to separate yourself in order to gain a bigger picture of life.

This transition means you have successfully moved outside of the shackles of living in the movement. You have gained a new superpower. But with great power comes great responsibility.

The research you've done, the people you've asked for help from, it's all built on those who have come before you. Sure, you're contributing your version to the long line of data, but we can't ignore the fact that your life and efforts are significantly easier through the efforts of millions who have come before you. I mean, you're not stomping through a forest to build a fire in a cave. You're reading a book right now, something our ancestors had limited success with, and you might even be reading it on a digital device. You have benefited (even if unknowingly) from the fruits of their labor.

The last step in being a student of impact, then, is realizing that you cannot take this learning for granted. Doing so would be adopting the same mentality of a child, assuming the world revolves around their single-dimensional needs.

As a student of impact you understand that the world needs constant improvement and renewal. While you may take time to gratify your impulses and consume what others have made, it is now your duty to contribute, make, carry forward your work, and serve the higher purpose to pass this knowledge on to those who follow you.

Only once you've taken that step will you move from being a student of impact, to being a master of impact.

ACKNOWLEDGMENTS

I'd like to thank Cassie Kozyrkov for providing so much of her time, detailing all the facets of the Decision Intelligence space. Not only did that improve the tone and direction of this book, but it also unearthed many tools for my own goals as well.

I'd like to thank my mentees and folks that I manage and mentor. They have let me test these theories on them countless times over the past decade (in many cases unknowingly). I hope this work has helped you achieve your goals.

ABOUT THE AUTHOR

COLT McANLIS is an engineer, mentor, consultant, and lover of pumpkin pie. As a developer advocate for Google, his content has helped more than 4.5 million developers learn to build better, cheaper, and more performant applications. Prior to Google, Colt was a graphics and performance engineer in the games industry for Microsoft's Ensemble Studios, Blizzard Entertainment, and Petroglyph Games. He has been an adjunct professor at Southern Methodist University and takes the opportunity to lecture at UCLA every now and again.

Made in United States
Troutdale, OR
02/28/2024

17980829R00152